RESEARCH WORKOUT

by
Harriet Hope Green
and
Dr. Sue Gillespie Martin

Illustrated by Gerald Melton

Cover by Gerald Melton
Copyright © Good Apple, Inc., 1984
ISBN No. 0-86653-194-7

Good Apple, Inc.
A Division of Frank Schaffer Publications, Inc.
23740 Hawthorne Boulevard,
Torrance, CA 90505-5927

DEDICATIONS

To my brother, Larry, who taught me the value of research and the rewards to be gleaned from it.

To my husband, Henry, with whom I celebrate twenty years of love and support.

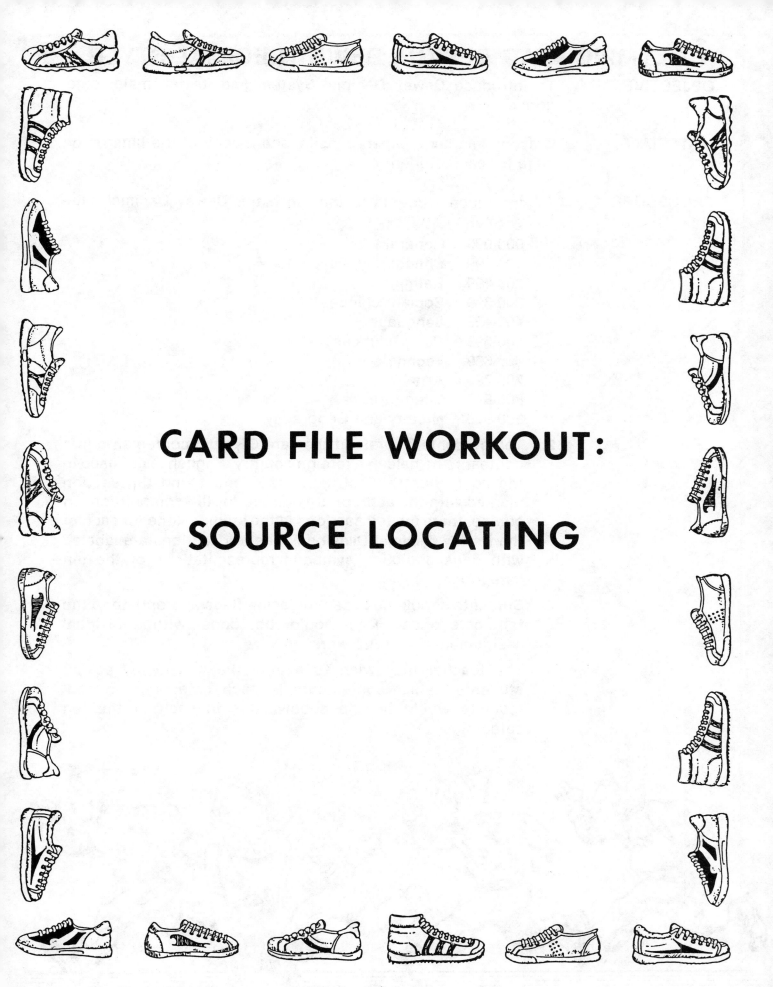

CARD FILE WORKOUT:

SOURCE LOCATING

OLYMPIC FLAG DESIGN: DEWEY DECIMAL STYLE

OBJECTIVE: To introduce Dewey Decimal System and its ten major categories.

MATERIALS: Crayons, markers, paper, pencils, and a copy of the illustration page for each student

PROCEDURE:

1. Introduce students to the ten major Dewey Decimal categories:

000-099	General Work
100-199	Philosophy, Psychology
200-299	Religion
300-399	Social Sciences
400-499	Language
500-599	Pure Sciences
600-699	Technology
700-799	Arts
800-899	Literature
900-999	History and Geography

2. Tell students to pretend they are Olympic contestants in a contest to be held in a foreign country. English is not used in the host country. Each competitor must find the section marked with the appropriate contest for the competition. Of course, there are ten sections in the stadium (one for each of the Dewey Decimal Divisions). The ten sections are labeled with flags depicting symbolic representations of the ten categories.

3. Students should be asked to design flags appropriate to the ten categories. This could be done with individual assignments or group work.

4. The teacher may wish to extend the activity by asking students to list contestants in each category; the contestants would be the subdivisions in each of the ten categories.

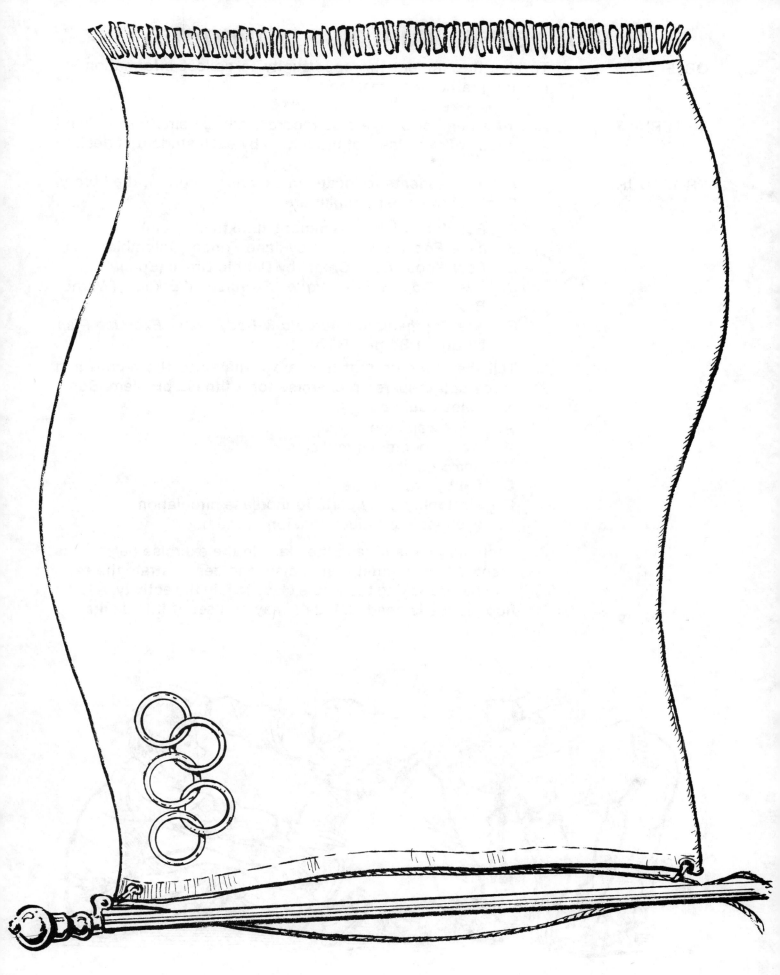

WONDERFUL WORLD OF WORKOUTS

OBJECTIVE: To give the student the opportunity to collect information via listening rather than reading.

MATERIALS: Any of a number of exercise records, a large empty room, and some type of exercise mat brought in by each student, if desired

PROCEDURE:

1. Ask the students to locate an exercise record at the library. Some of the most popular are:

   A. *Reach* by Richard Simmons (Elektra/Asylum)
   B. *Jane Fonda's Workout* by Jane Fonda (Columbia)
   C. *Feel Good! Look Great!* by Debbie Drake (Epic)
   D. *Miss Piggy's Aerobique Exercise Workout* (Warner Brothers)
   E. *The Southampton Aerobic & Body Toner Exercise Plan* by Stuart Berger (RCA)

2. Tell the students that they are to listen to the record and study and prepare an exercise for a fitness problem. Some examples could be:

   A. thick waistlines
   B. weak abdominal muscles
   C. heavy thighs
   D. flabby upper arms
   E. stretching body parts to increase circulation
   F. exercises to reduce tension in the body

3. Each student is to lead the class in the exercise he/she has prepared. Each must first explain and demonstrate the exercise before asking the whole class to join the activity. A large floor space is needed. Music may be used if it is desirable.

CIRCLING THE FIELD

OBJECTIVE: To help students understand the purposes and potential uses of cross-references when doing research.

MATERIALS: A variety of materials from students' homes having to do with sports or fitness (stopwatch, bats, balls, etc.), index cards, large table, pencils

PROCEDURE:

1. Explain to students that cross-references are tools that often help a researcher direct attention to additional information about a topic. Please include the following ideas in the discussion:

   A. Cross-references are used in many types of materials including dictionaries, thesaurus, encyclopedia, *Readers' Guide,* etc.

   B. Cross-references can be called "Related Ideas," "See also," etc.

2. To illustrate an example, the teacher might encourage the students to find the word "Sports" in an encyclopedia. There are generally many cross-references under that heading.

3. Ask each student to bring a sports or fitness-related item from home—balls, bats, shoes, sweat suit, etc. As the items are brought to class, display them on a large table.

4. Number each display item randomly, and place corresponding number in the corner of an index card.

5. Distribute numbered cards to students, and ask each student to write four or five cross-reference clues for the item numbered on the card. Remind students NOT to name the item, but rather to write CLUES. For example, cross-reference clues for running shoes might be jogging, marathon running, and long-distance running.

6. Collect the index cards and read cross-reference clues to the class to see who can identify the most items from clues alone.

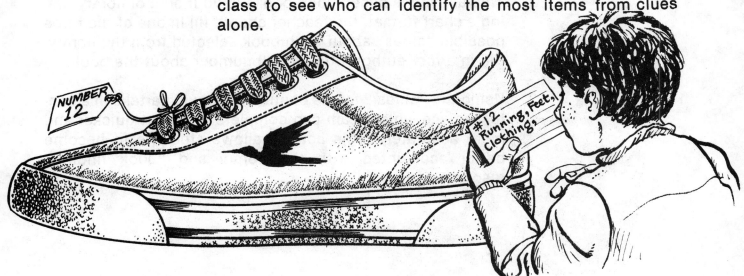

CARD CATALOGUE HAT TRICK

OBJECTIVES:

1. To familiarize students with the card catalogue and the Dewey Decimal System.

2. To help students understand the uses and functions of subject, author and title cards.

MATERIALS:

Paper, pencil, a variety of current reference materials like newspapers and current magazines, 8½ × 11 construction paper

PROCEDURE:

Feat I

1. Discuss the purpose of title, author and subject cards with the students. Be sure to include ideas like:

    Title card: omits determiners in the title; the title appears on first line, whereas the author appears on the second.

    Author card: author's last name first; the title of book appears under author's name.

    Subject card: subject usually in capital letters; sometimes cross-reference follows subject.

2. Ask each student to read an article from a current reference source (newspaper or magazine) about fitness or sports.

3. Ask each student to make an author, title and subject card (including cross-references) for the article as if it were a book. Students may wish to use appropriate call numbers as well.

4. A class card catalogue could then be assembled.

Feat II

1. This activity is based upon books in your school library. Using a chart format, the teacher should fill in one of the three possible "clues" about each book selected from the library. Fill in *either* author, title, or call number about the book.

2. Using the "clues," teams of students could partake in a contest to see which team can complete the chart quicker and more accurately. This activity allows students to become better acquainted with the library and "book finding" resources.

Feat III

1. Prepare sheets of 8½ × 11 paper with one Dewey Decimal number on each sheet (at least one sheet for every student in the class). Write these numbers in sets, so they might be found on one shelf in the library. (Example: 801.12 AB, 801.12 C, 802.13, 802.13C, 802.23, etc.)

2. Mix each set, and divide students into groups of six. Give each group one number set, and give each individual one card from the set.

3. The group members then "become" books and must arrange themselves on the shelf in proper order.

4. Have a contest to see which group can arrange themselves in proper order first.

5. Students may wish to make additional cards using books and call numbers from the school library.

ABC'S OF WATER SPORT TRIVIA

OBJECTIVE: To give students experiences with alphabetizing.

MATERIALS: Pencils, paper and exercise below to be duplicated

PROCEDURE:
1. Ask students to alphabetize the list of words above each paragraph. Then, each list should be numbered (after it is alphabetized) beginning with the *A* words. Then each numbered word can be placed in the paragraph in place of its corresponding number.

2. When this is complete, students may wish to produce their own paragraphs.

Paragraph I

crawl	arm
butterfly	kicks
swimming	backstroke
sport	basic
strokes	water
breaststroke	

(10) _____ is a (8) _____

in which one moves through the (11) _____

by (7) _____ and (1) _____

(9) _____. Competition is usually based

upon four (3) _____ strokes: (2) _____,

(4)_____, (5)_____, and

(6) _____. Swimming is one of the oldest

sports of all.

Paragraph II

handle	caught
competition	length
time	ride
surfers	ability
based	surfer
judged	waves

Surfing is the sport of riding (12) _____ on a

surfboard. (4) _____ is (2) _____ upon

the number of waves a (9)_____ can ride within a

period of (11) _____. (10) _____ are (6) _____

on how soon the wave is (3) _____, and (7) _____

of the (8) _____ and the (1) _____ to

(5)_____the board.

8

Paragraph III

however	snorkelers
air	scuba
skin	divers
all	mask
fins	underwater
basic	

Skin divers can be called (10)_____ or (8)_____ divers. (2)_____ (9)_____ (4)_____ explore the (11)_____. Divers who use only the (3)_____ equipment like a (7)_____, (5)_____ and a snorkel are called snorkelers. (6)_____, people who use (1)_____ are called scuba divers.

Paragraph IV

goalkeepers	goal
opponents	area
dribble	rectangular
dribbled	polo
player	moved
hockey	crawl

Water (11)_____ is played with two teams of seven (10)_____ in a (12)_____ (1)_____ or pool. The ball is (8)_____ or (4)_____ and passed from one player to another. Usually, players (3)_____a ball by using a (2)_____. The object of the game is to move the ball past the (9)_____ (5)_____. Like (7)_____, water polo teams have (6)_____.

TIME MACHINE SPORTS PROBE

OBJECTIVE: To exercise question-asking skills by means of probing.

MATERIALS: Time cards on page 11 and a time machine fashioned out of found sports objects

PROCEDURE:

1. Have the class members contribute to the construction of a time machine by bringing a sports item from home, such as an old tennis shoe, a baseball cap, a program, a stopwatch, etc. Encourage the imaginative arrangement of the items to fashion a time machine. Put the time cards in the construction.

2. One at a time, each student is asked to draw a time card with a sports name written on it from the time machine.

3. The student will pretend to be the figure whose name is written on the time card while the rest of the class probes for the correct identity by asking questions. Questions are to be answered "yes," "no," or "I don't know" in order to require the interviewer to *probe* deeper. Try to get more and more specific information with each question.

   SAMPLE PROBE

   A. Are you a male sports figure?
   B. Are you alive?
   C. Did you play a team sport?
   D. Are you an American sports figure?
   E. Did you compete in the Olympics?
   F. Did you win a gold medal?
   G. Did you win more than one gold medal?
   H. Did you win more than three gold medals?
   I. Are you a swimmer?
   J. Is your name Mark Spitz?

4. The procedure continues until all class members have had the opportunity to be both an interviewer and an interviewee.

BILL RODGERS

1. American long-distance runner
2. Living
3. Set a Boston Marathon record in 1975 at 2 hours, 9 minutes, and 55 seconds
4. By 1981 Rodgers had won eighteen marathon titles.

JOE NAMATH

1. Football player
2. Living
3. Quarterback for New York Jets
4. Nicknamed "Broadway Joe"

DOROTHY HAMILL

1. United States figure skater
2. Living
3. Won gold medal for figure skating in 1976 Winter Olympics
4. Known for her wedge haircut

BABE RUTH

1. Baseball player
2. Dead
3. Hit 714 home runs in his career
4. The 240 lb. pitcher played for a number of teams including the Yankees.

BABE DIDRIKSON ZAHARIAS

1. Greatest United States woman athlete
2. Dead
3. Winner of 1932 national women's track and field records in javelin, high jump, and hurdles
4. One of the greatest women golfers

MUHAMMAD ALI

1. American boxer
2. Living
3. 1964 heavyweight champion who wrote a piece of doggerel before each fight
4. Changed his name from Cassius Clay when he joined the Nation of Islam

JESSE OWENS

1. American Negro runner and jumper
2. Dead
3. Won four gold medals at 1936 Olympics
4. His winning of the 100 meters infuriated Hitler due to the fact that he was black.

JIM THORPE

1. American Indian
2. Dead
3. Won the decathlon and the pentathlon in 1918 Olympics
4. Medals taken away until 1983 because he played professional football

1972 OLYMPIC GAMES MURAL

OBJECTIVE: To investigate the use of the *Readers' Guide to Periodical Literature* as an informational source.

MATERIALS: *Readers' Guide*, butcher paper, and markers

PROCEDURES:

1. Tell the class that they are going to draw a mural depicting the events at the 1972 Olympic Games in Munich. Sources for information must be pulled from the *Readers' Guide to Periodical Literature*, March 1972-February 1973.

2. Encourage the students to read as many accounts of the 1972 Winter Games as they can find listed including those in *Sports Illustrated, Newsweek, Time, Reader's Digest, Nation,* and *Life.*

3. Ask the class to divide itself into interest groups for the drawing of events based on their research. Important interest groups should include: the terrorist attack on Jewish athletes, U.S. yachting competition, ouster of Rhodesia, Mark Spitz's gold medals, and Cathy Rigby's record.

INDEXING THE CONTENTS OF A SPORTING GOODS STORE

OBJECTIVE: To help students understand how to use a table of contents and index as tools in doing research.

MATERIALS: A science or social studies textbook for all students, paper, pencil, markers or crayons, drawing paper

PROCEDURE:

1. Have students examine their textbooks (either science or social studies). After finding the table of contents and index, discuss some generalizations about each tool. Be sure to include:

    A. the location of each tool in the book.
    B. the table of contents is divided into units and chapters that are listed in page number order.
    C. the table of contents is generalized, includes chapter titles, and page numbers.
    D. the index is in alphabetical order and also includes page numbers.
    E. the index listings are very specific.

2. Once students understand the differences, ask the children to imagine they just purchased a huge sporting goods store. The store is arranged in aisles according to individual sports. For example, ski equipment is in one aisle, baseball in another, etc. Allow students to select eight or ten sports in which to "specialize."

3. Divide the class into groups of two or three so that each group can work on a shopping guide for the new store. One group must make a "table of contents" for the store, labeling each aisle and dividing each aisle into general subdivisions (units and chapters). For example, Aisle I might be tennis and general subdivisions might include clothing, equipment, sundries, etc. The other groups of students will each be assigned one specific aisle and must first brainstorm all items that might be found on the shelf, and then "index" these specifics for shoppers. Remind the students that an index must be in alphabetical order.

4. Students may wish to illustrate the guide when they are done.

BE A LIST MAKER

OBJECTIVE: To give the student the opportunity to use popular reference material as a source for creativity.

MATERIALS: *Book of Lists #2* by Irving Wallace, David Walleckinsky, Amy Wallace, Sylvia Wallace (Bantam), paper, pencils, and a very long scroll

PROCEDURE:
1. Ask the students to divide themselves into groups of four. Each group should make a list of the twenty-six lists concerning sports published in the *Book of Lists #2.*

2. Each group should then brainstorm in order to come up with ideas for four sports lists. For instance, ideas could be:
   A. The Ten Best-Selling Running Shoes as compiled by a local sports retailer
   B. The Ten Worst Defeats (suffered by one of the school's teams) as compiled by one of the school's coaches
   C. The Ten Most Popular Sports Biographies as compiled by the school's librarian or a local bookstore

   Encourage the groups to compile four lists that have a balance between serious and frivolous content. In other words, do not allow all four lists from each group to be crazy.

3. Have all of the groups write out their lists on a long scroll paper, creating a huge list of lists.

ALPHABETIZING TWOSOME

OBJECTIVES:
1. To give students experiences in alphabetizing lists of words.
2. To prepare students for using reference materials that are in alphabetical order.

MATERIALS:
Any portable gym equipment available in your building (soccer balls, baseballs, bats, ropes, nets, sticks, etc.), chalkboard space, dictionaries, paper and pencil, books about sports (optional)

PROCEDURE:

Part I

1. Place all portable gym equipment on a table, and ask students to name each item. As students name each piece, the teacher should be listing names of equipment on the board.

2. Ask students to name other types of gym material (spikes, nets, fields, bases, etc.) as teacher lists these words on the board.

3. When list is complete, allow students to "compete" to see who can be the first to accurately alphabetize the list.

Part II

1. Write the following "sports" words on the board, or place them on a ditto for each student. (Do not include definitions.)
   A. ROUNDERS - game similar to baseball; popular in Britain
   B. FALCONRY - training, keeping, and hunting falcons or eagles
   C. QUOITS - game similar to horseshoes
   D. BALACLAVA - head covering with openings for eyes and mouth; used by skiers and mountain climbers
   E. SPELUNKING - sport of exploring caves
   F. ROQUET - similar to croquet; played with short mallots.
   G. KABOOM - trampoline stunt
   H. KAYO - to knock out opponent in boxing
   I. CODY - trampoline stunt
   J. SCOW - type of boat with flat bottom
   K. FINESSE - delicate skill allowing you to win
   L. BOCCI - Italian bowling game

2. Teacher should divide students into teams of two; each team needs a dictionary. Teacher could randomly call out one word at a time to see which team can locate it first in the dictionary.

3. After the dictionary "warm-up," ask teams to alphabetize the list, look up each word, and write or illustrate the definition to make a sports dictionary.

4. Teacher may wish to have students add to their dictionary as they do other activities in fitness training.

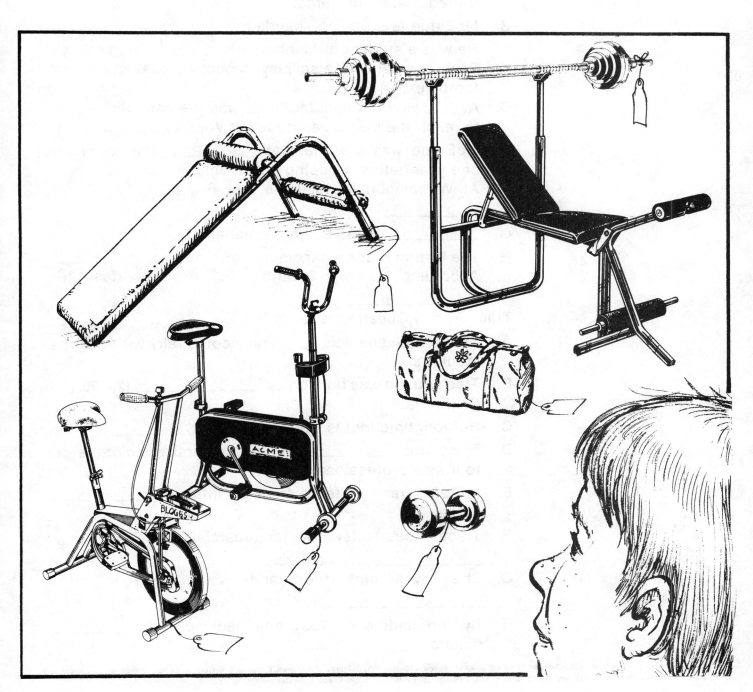

SPOTLIGHTING SPORTS

OBJECTIVE: To learn how to use *Current Biography* to locate information on particular personalities.

MATERIALS: Set of *Current Biography* and set of questions to be answered

PROCEDURE:
1. Tell the class that they are to use *Current Biography* to obtain certain pieces of biographical information. Be sure not to reveal the location by year of each personality. Ask the students to look the name up in the index.

2. John McEnroe Questionnaire
   A. McEnroe was born in _____, West Germany, where his father was stationed as a member of the United States Air Force.
   B. McEnroe is _____ handed.
   C. He was a student at Manhattan's _____ High School, where he also played soccer, basketball, and football.
   D. At ____ years of age, McEnroe was the youngest player to reach the men's semifinals at Wimbledon.
   E. McEnroe was a student at _____ University for one year before dropping out of school.
   F. At Wimbledon in 1980, he lost 6-1, 5-7, 3-6, 7-6, 6-8 to _____.
   G. _____ is his business manager.
   H. The British Press nicknamed McEnroe _____.
   I. According to Tony Palafox, McEnroe's greatest gift is _____.

3. Tracy Austin Questionnaire
   A. By the time she was ____, Tracy could rally with college students.
   B. Tracy Austin was born on _____ 12, 1962, in California.
   C. Her longtime idol is Chris _____.
   D. Tracy won _____ during her first six months on tour as a professional.
   E. In 1981 Tracy suffered from an inflamed _____ nerve.
   F. Tracy does television commercials for _____ _____ camera.
   G. She loves junk food and is addicted to mint _____.
   H. By the middle of 1981 she had won _____ dollars.

McEnroe answers as found in 1980 volume of *Current Biography*. A. Wiesbaden; B. left; C. Trinity; D. eighteen; E. Stanford; F. Borg; G. Father; H. Superbrat; I. concentration
Austin answers as found in 1981 *Current Biography*. A. 5; B. December; C. Evert; D. $173,000; E. sciatic; F. Canon AE-1; G. ice cream; H. one million

18

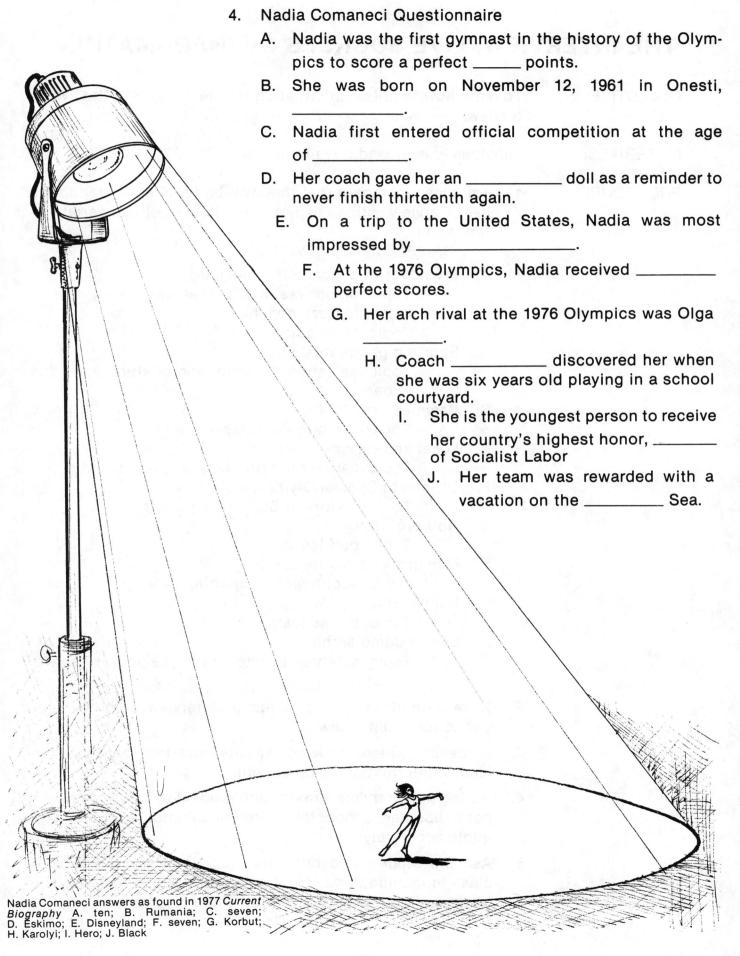

4. Nadia Comaneci Questionnaire

A. Nadia was the first gymnast in the history of the Olympics to score a perfect _____ points.

B. She was born on November 12, 1961 in Onesti, _____.

C. Nadia first entered official competition at the age of _____.

D. Her coach gave her an _____ doll as a reminder to never finish thirteenth again.

E. On a trip to the United States, Nadia was most impressed by _____.

F. At the 1976 Olympics, Nadia received _____ perfect scores.

G. Her arch rival at the 1976 Olympics was Olga _____.

H. Coach _____ discovered her when she was six years old playing in a school courtyard.

I. She is the youngest person to receive her country's highest honor, _____ of Socialist Labor

J. Her team was rewarded with a vacation on the _____ Sea.

Nadia Comaneci answers as found in 1977 *Current Biography* A. ten; B. Rumania; C. seven; D. Eskimo; E. Disneyland; F. seven; G. Korbut; H. Karolyi; I. Hero; J. Black

19

THE INTERVIEW: LIVE SOURCES OF INFORMATION

OBJECTIVE: To learn how to obtain information via the process of the live interview.

MATERIALS: Individually designed questionnaires

PROCEDURE:

1. Tell class members that they will be required to conduct a live interview with an expert in the field to obtain certain information.

   SAMPLE INTERVIEWEES

   A. President of a local Little League
      Topic: objectives of Little League
   B. High school football coach
      Topic: team spirit
   C. Sporting goods retailer
      Topic: selection of proper sports attire, including shoes
   D. Baseball umpire
      Topic: evolution of rules
   E. Local sportscaster
      Topic: career opportunities in sportscasting
   F. Official of Special Olympics
      Topic: history of Special Olympics
   G. Golf professional
      Topic: golf lessons
   H. Manager of a sports arena
      Topic: economics of sporting events
   I. Fitness doctor
      Topic: stress tests
   J. Sports dome architect
      Topic: safety as a factor in the designing of sports structures

2. Have each class member select an interviewee and write or phone for an interview.

3. Ask each student to design twenty questions based on the kind of information being sought.

4. During the interview remind each student to be on time, be a good listener, probe for more meaningful answers, and quote accurately.

5. Ask the students to bring the questions and answers to class to include in a booklet entitled *Sports Interviews.* The booklet should have a cover and some illustrations.

PHOTO-FINISH EXERCISE

OBJECTIVES:
1. To introduce students to picture and pamphlet files in the library.
2. To make students aware of potential uses for these tools.

MATERIALS: Instant camera, film, paper, pencil, newspapers and magazines for cutting, glue, scissors

PROCEDURE:

1. Have students examine both the picture and pamphlet files in the library. Discuss the types of materials found in each file, and discuss the student observations about each file. Be sure to include ideas like:

   A. Both files are in alphabetical order by subject.
   B. Pictures and pamphlets cannot be cut or pasted.
   C. Pamphlet files contain booklets, bulletins, and leaflets usually published by organizations, companies, or governments.
   D. Pamphlets are short and usually deal with one subject.

2. Discuss with students the potential uses of pictures and pamphlets in research.

3. Divide students into groups of four or five. Each group is to pretend it is the Principal's Advisory Council on Health and Fitness and must "publish" a pamphlet about the fitness program in the school. The pamphlet should be geared for the student body and should include photographs planned and taken by group members. Research can be done in the library, and perhaps the gym teacher and principal could be interviewed for quotes. Pamphlets could be shared with other classes in the building.

4. (Optional) If the teacher wishes to reinforce the introduction to the picture file, a fitness bulletin board could be displayed. Ask groups of students to make collages on poster board by using magazines or newspapers. Each collage could reflect a theme like winter sports, summer sports, equipment, exercise, etc.

SPORTS GO TO THE MOVIES

OBJECTIVE: To give students the opportunity to use partial information to locate complete information.

MATERIALS: A list of sports movies and the dates when they were released, poster board, markers, and a variety of movie encyclopedias, Hollywood dictionaries, and a *Who's Who in Film Publications*

PROCEDURE:

1. Ask the class to divide itself into pairs. Give each pair the list of fifteen sports movies and the dates of their releases. The list could include:

   A. *The Champion* (1949).
   B. *Fear Strikes Out* (1957).
   C. *Brian's Song* (1971)
   D. *Damn Yankees* (1958)
   E. *Bang the Drums Slowly* (1973)
   F. *Knute Rockne, All American* (1940)
   G. *Chariots of Fire* (1981)
   H. *The Babe Ruth Story* (1948)
   I. *Somebody Up There Likes Me* (1956)
   J. *Follow the Sun* (1951)
   K. *The Bob Mathias Story* (1954)
   L. *The Longest Run* (1970)
   M. *Jim Thorpe, All American* (1951)
   N. *Rocky* (1976)
   O. *Fat City* (1972)

2. Tell the pairs to go to film encyclopedias and Hollywood dictionaries and look up all fifteen titles and record who starred in each film, what sport each film was about, and what studio made each film.

3. Finally, the students, working in pairs, are to then design a publicity poster for one of the movies using their research. Markers and poster board should be used.

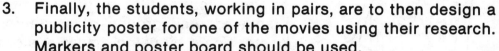

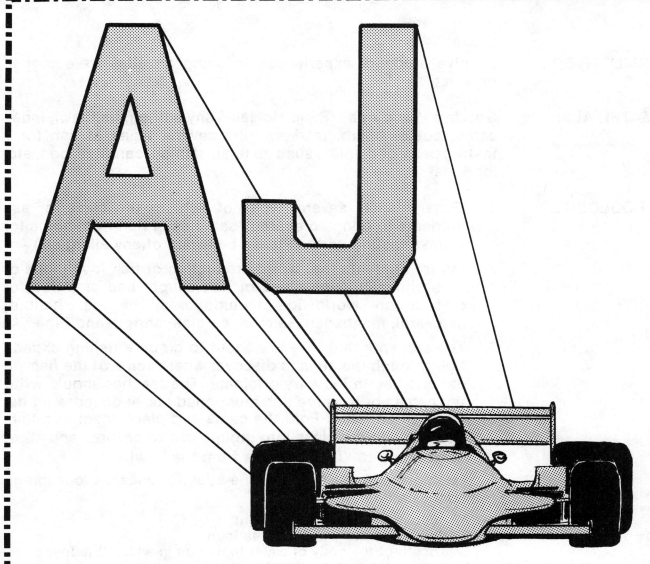

The A.J. Foyt Story

AN AMERICAN TRADITION

○ GASOLINE ALLEY FILMS PRESENTATION ○

WALDO NEWMAN ·· WANDA HICKEY
GARY GREASERAG ·· MILO BUNTS
AND CHRIS ECONOMACKY

| PG | PARENTAL GUIDANCE   SUGGESTED | 🌐 |

DIRECTED BY LUCAS GEORGE | ▷◁ | DOLBY STEREO |
PRODUCED BY CLYDE MEGGABUX

Ⓒ 1993

CATCH OF THE DAY

OBJECTIVE: To give students experiences in using an atlas as a tool in research.

MATERIALS: *Goode's World Atlas* (Rand McNally) any edition, fishbowl, index cards, poster board, markers, and several types of fish for a tasting party or display, such as tuna, salmon, sardines, cod, etc. (optional)

PROCEDURE:

1. Either display several types of fish for the class, or ask students to bring "prepared" samples of fish from home for a class tasting party. (Please be aware of any allergies.)

2. Inform students that world production of fish is millions of tons annually. Nine types of fish caught and prepared for distribution worldwide include cod, herring, halibut, mackerel, menhaden, salmon, sardine, shrimp and tuna.

3. Tell students that they are about to go on a fishing expedition through the atlas to discover where some of the fish we eat and use in industry originate. The teacher should write the names of the nine fish mentioned above on index cards, one fish per card. Fold the cards and place them in a fishbowl. Divide the class into groups of two or three and allow each group to "fish" a name from the bowl.

4. Each group must then use the atlas to research four things about its "catch":

   A. country in which it is caught
   B. body of water in which it is found
   C. depth of the body of water in meters in which it is found
   D. continent in which fish is caught

5. The teacher could then set up a large graph like the one pictured on page 25 and allow the students to fill in the information on the graph.

6. Optional: students may be encouraged to find pictures of their "catch," and a bulletin board could be displayed.

24

FISH	CONTINENT	COUNTRY	BODY OF WATER	DEPTH
COD				
SALMON				
TUNA				
SARDINE				
SHRIMP				
MENHADEN				
HALIBUT				
MACKEREL				
HERRING				

SPORTS STORIES IN TABLEAU

OBJECTIVE: To give students the opportunity to locate information in the *New York Times Index* and on microfilm.

MATERIALS: *New York Times Index* for 1981, microfilms, and appropriate props gathered by students to erect the sports tableau

PROCEDURE:

1. Direct the students, in groups of three, to go to the 1981 *New York Times Index* and look up one of the following assigned sports stories published in the *New York Times* during 1981. Tell the students to look under Baseball for the articles. Do not reveal the dates as shown in parentheses.

   A. Los Angeles Dodgers' pitcher Fernando Valenzuela is voted NL's rookie of the year. (D.3, IV, 21:5)

   B. Bob Gibson elected to Hall of Fame. Story by Red Smith. (Ja. 16, 17:1)

   C. Len Barker pitches perfect game against Toronto. (My. 16, 17:1)

   D. Marvin Miller announces that players are on strike. (Je. 12, 1:5)

   E. Players' strike ends; season will resume August 9; some owners and players comment. (Ag. 1, 1:1)

   F. Pete Rose breaks Stan Musial's National League record for career hits with 3,631. (Ag. 12, 26:1)

   G. New York Yankees win AL championship. (O.16, 25:6)

   H. Los Angeles wins NL pennant. (O. 20, 25:6)

   I. Tom Seaver becomes fifth pitcher to reach 5,000 career strikeouts. (Ap. 19, V, 6:1)

   J. Ted Giannoulas wears eight-foot chicken costume to baseball games in attempt to add comic relief for fans. (Je. 30, III, 11:1)

   K. Three hundred thirty workers strike Hillerich & Bradley Co., which produces about 90% of Louisville slugger bats. (Ap. 16, IV, 4:1)

   L. New York Superstar Baseball Card Show to open in Manhattan. (Mr. 23, II, 8:3)

2. Ask each group to pull the appropriately dated microfilm and read the assigned story for the facts and details of the event.

3. Each group should then create a sports story tableau depicting the assigned event. Props and costumes should be brought from home.

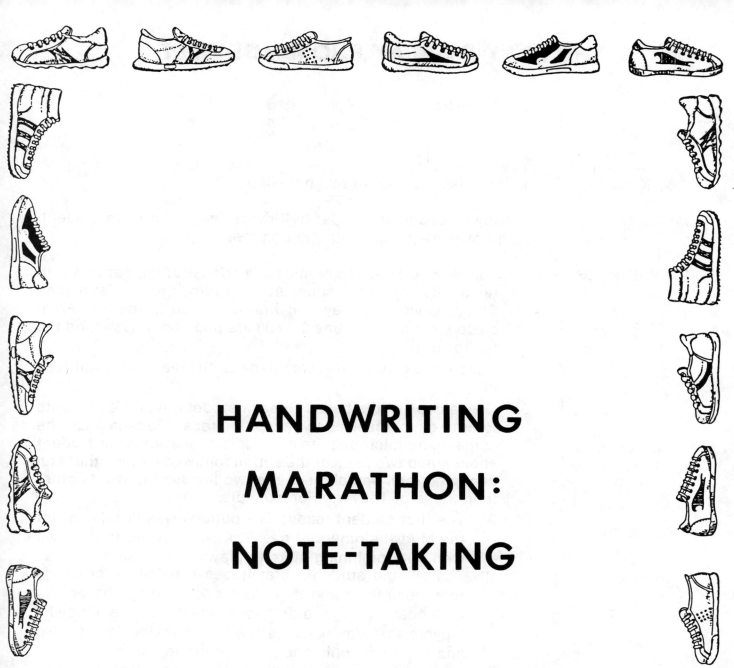

HANDWRITING MARATHON: NOTE-TAKING

THE PLAY BY PLAY FROM MUDVILLE

OBJECTIVE: To exercise the skill of paraphrasing.

MATERIALS: A copy of *Casey at the Bat* by Ernest Thayer for each student, audio cassettes, tape and microphones

PROCEDURES:
1. Tell the class that the comic ballad *Casey at the Bat* was written in 1888 by a philosophy student turned journalist named Ernest Lawrence Thayer. It first appeared in the *San Francisco Examiner* on June 3, 1888. Its popularity has stood the test of time.

2. Read the ballad on the next page to the class with full feeling.

3. Give a copy of the ballad to each student. Ask the students to arrange themselves in pairs and prepare to broadcast the game using microphones and audio cassettes. One student should read two lines of the action followed by the other student who then paraphrases the two lines using words other than those of Thayers. For example:

   A. The first student reads "The outlook wasn't brilliant for the Mudville nine that day. The score stood four to two with but one inning more to play."

   B. The second student paraphrases it using other words that mean the same thing as those used by Thayer. For instance: "Things didn't look good for the Mudville players that day because they were losing four to two and there was only one more inning to play."

4. This should be continued until each pair reading and then paraphrasing completes the taping of the entire poem. Each pair should play the tape back in order to hear how well it was read and paraphrased.

CASEY AT THE BAT

The outlook wasn't brilliant for the Mudville nine that day;
The score stood four to two with but one inning more to play.
And then when Cooney died at first, and Barrows did the same,
A sickly silence fell upon the patrons of the game.

A straggling few got up to go in deep despair. The rest
Clung to that hope which springs eternal in the human breast;
They thought if only Casey could but get a whack at that—
We'd put up even money now with Casey at the bat.

But Flynn preceded Casey, as did also Jimmy Black,
And the former was a lulu and the latter was a cake;
So upon that stricken multitude grim melancholy sat,
For there seemed but little chance of Casey's getting to the bat.

But Flynn let drive a single, to the wonderment of all,
And Blake, the much despised, tore the cover off the ball;
And when the dust had lifted, and the men saw what had occurred,
There was Johnnie safe at second and Flynn a-hugging third.

Then from 5,000 throats and more there rose a lusty yell;
It rumbled through the valley, it rattled in the dell;
It knocked upon the mountain and recoiled upon the flat,
For Casey, mighty Casey, was advancing to the bat.

There was ease in Casey's manner as he stepped into his place;
There was pride in Casey's bearing and a smile on Casey's face.
And when, responding to the cheers, he lightly doffed his hat,
No stranger in the crowd could doubt 'twas Casey at the bat.

Ten thousand eyes were on him as he rubbed his hands with dirt;
Five thousand tongues applauded when he wiped them on his shirt.
Then while the writhing pitcher ground the ball into his hip,
Defiance gleamed in Casey's eye, a sneer curled Casey's lip.

And now the leather-covered sphere came hurling through the air,
And Casey stood a-watching it in haughty grandeur there.
Close by the sturdy batsman the ball unheeded sped—
"That ain't my style," said Casey. "Strike one," the umpire said.

From the benches, black with people, there went up a muffled roar,
Like the beating of the storm-waves on a stern and distant shore.
"Kill him! Kill the umpire!" shouted someone in the stand;
And it's likely they'd have killed him had not Casey raised his hand.

With a smile of Christian charity great Casey's visage shone;
He stilled the rising tumult; he bade the game go on;
He signaled to the pitcher, and once more the spheroid flew;
But Casey still ignored it, and the umpire said "Strike two."

"Fraud!" cried the maddened thousands, and echo answered fraud;
But one scornful look from Casey and the audience was awed.
They saw his face grow stern and cold, they saw his muscles strain,
And they knew that Casey wouldn't let that ball go by again.

The sneer is gone from Casey's lip, his teeth are clenched in hate;
He pounds with cruel violence his bat upon the plate.
And now the pitcher holds the ball, and now he lets it go,
And now the air is shattered by the force of Casey's blow.

Oh, somewhere in this favoured land the sun is shining bright;
The band is playing somewhere, and somewhere hearts are light,
And somewhere men are laughing, and somewhere children shout;
But there is no joy in Mudville—mighty Casey has struck out.

SPORTSCASTING LIMITED

OBJECTIVE: To help students locate and focus upon the main idea in research materials.

MATERIALS: Large open area in the classroom, several sports pages from recent newspapers, a microphone, paper, pencil, tape recorder

PROCEDURE:

1. Divide students into groups of three or four. Ask each group to think of a sport or fitness activity to mime in front of the group. Teacher may wish to encourage students to mime unusual sports like kite flying, helicopter racing, etc.

2. Ask each group to present its mime while others try to guess the sport.

3. Once everyone has had a turn, point out to students that they were using visual clues to help them determine a main idea. Discuss clues using various groups' presentations as examples.

4. Discuss main idea with students. Point out that many people like umpires, writers, etc., in the world of sports use visual clues to determine main ideas. When we watch a sports event on television, we use both visual and auditory clues.

5. Tell students that today the class is going to present a live sports news radio broadcast. Each person is going to be a newscaster and will present one item of interest from the newspapers available in the classroom. The teacher should assign one article to each student. However, due to commitments made to advertisers, the broadcast must be limited to twenty seconds per reporter. Therefore, each student must report ONLY main ideas to the audience.

6. Allow time for students to read articles and pull main ideas.

7. Tape-record the broadcast as each student does a twenty-second presentation, and play the tape for everyone.

INFERRING A CROSSWORD PUZZLE

OBJECTIVE: To help students develop and use inference skills.

MATERIALS: Crossword puzzle on the next page, pencil, paper, and a thesaurus and sports dictionary (optional)

PROCEDURE:
1. Discuss "inference" with students pointing out that we all infer things daily. For example, if we wake up and hear on the radio that the temperature is 0°C, we infer that we must wear warm clothes. When we infer, we use clues to formulate conclusions.
2. We use this skill when we do crossword puzzles. Present the crossword puzzle to the students and tell them that they will be using inference skills to fill in the answers.
3. Once students have completed the puzzle, encourage them to make their own crossword puzzles by dividing the class into groups of two or three. Challenge each group to make a puzzle that revolves around a theme like sports equipment, medicine, a certain sport, or a famous sports figure.
4. Have groups exchange puzzles and attempt to complete one anothers' games.

32

ACROSS

1.   a.   equipment
     b.   used in tennis and squash
     c.   used to hit a ball
2.   a.   noun
     b.   games or sports of athletes
     c.   activity in exercise
3.   a.   sport
     b.   done on ice or water
     c.   requires hills or boat
4.   a.   man or woman
     b.   needs alley, ball and pins
     c.   often plays with team
5.   a.   helps indicate time
     b.   is equipment
     c.   required for timed races
6.   a.   can be a verb or noun
     b.   athletes try to do this
     c.   given medals for it

DOWN

1.   a.   used by runners often
     b.   can be flat or hilly
     c.   trains move on it
2.   a.   game
     b.   requires court, ball, net
     c.   Harlem Globetrotters
3.   a.   sport
     b.   cross between run and walk
     c.   good exercise
4.   a.   contest
     b.   series of games
     c.   losers eliminated
5.   a.   sport
     b.   always done in water
     c.   different strokes
6.   a.   base on balls
     b.   can force in run
     c.   four bad pitches

IS THAT A FACT?

OBJECTIVE: To give students an opportunity to use both fact and opinion in their research, reading, and writing.

MATERIALS: Pencils, scissors, the sports sections from several local newspapers, newspaper ads for sports or fitness items

PROCEDURE:

1. Discuss the difference between a fact and an opinion with students. Try to include ideas like:

   A. A fact can be substantiated by checking other research materials. Facts can be used to support opinions. An example of a fact would be "The score of the soccer game was 5-3."

   B. An opinion includes feelings, thoughts, beliefs, claims. Opinions often include words like *better, more, think, feel, believe,* etc. An example of an opinion might be "Our soccer team is the best."

2. Ask students to give examples of facts and opinions.

3. Divide the class in half, each half to represent a different school. The two fictitious schools have just completed a soccer tournament against each other. Both groups should be given just one fact: "The score of the soccer game was 5-3." Assign students a "school" and ask them to write an article for their school newspaper describing the "game." Encourage students to embellish the 5-3 score with opinions and viewpoints.

4. Have students share their articles with the class to see how viewpoints are slanted when using opinions to justify facts.

5. Examine the sports section of a local newspaper to find opinionated words and phrases that might be different in another team's locale.

6. Encourage students to examine sports ads to find both facts and opinions.

7. The teacher may wish to use a bulletin board; divide it in half and label half FACTS and half OPINIONS. Students could then clip headlines from the sports page to place on the appropriate side of the bulletin board.

MAPPING THE BOGTOWN MARATHON

OBJECTIVE: To develop the ability to read maps for scientific information.

MATERIALS: Map of the Bogtown Marathon course, biology paper, and colored paper

PROCEDURE:

1. Tell the class that the famous Boston Marathon is considered by all to be the most difficult long-distance run in the world. Twenty-six miles long, it requires runners to go up and down over miles of rolling terrain. It is also the oldest footrace in America with the first race being held in 1897. The Bogtown Marathon is full of some of the same difficulties as the Boston Marathon.

2. Be sure to draw the students' attention to the legend at the bottom of the Bogtown Marathon map on the following pages. Tell them that by looking at the legend they can better understand the story the map has to tell including the scale to which it is drawn.

3. Give each student a copy of the map. Ask each student to read the map and answer the following questions:

    A. How many miles is it from the starting point at Hoppington to Trotley?

    B. What lake is near Roundalake Road?

    C. What street do the runners turn onto at least twice?

    D. What building is near Last Street at the end of the race?

    E. What island is closest to Groaner Hills?

    F. How many miles is it from Runner's Rock to the city limits of Thirston?

    G. What lake is near Owdatown?

    H. What route joins 60 at Determination City?

    I. Workout Trail runs through what green area?

    J. What route is also known as Brotherhood Freeway?

    K. The starting point of the race is at what cross streets in Hoppington?

    L. What is the largest body of water on this map?

    M. How many miles long is the Bogtown Marathon?

    N. What route does Crawley Road intersect?

4. Using the map on the illustration page, biology paper and colored pencils, ask each student to draw to scale a map of the Bogtown Marathon.

5. Have each student write in paragraph form a set of directions that gives the exact route of the Bogtown Marathon from Hoppington to the finish line.

The Bogtown Marathon

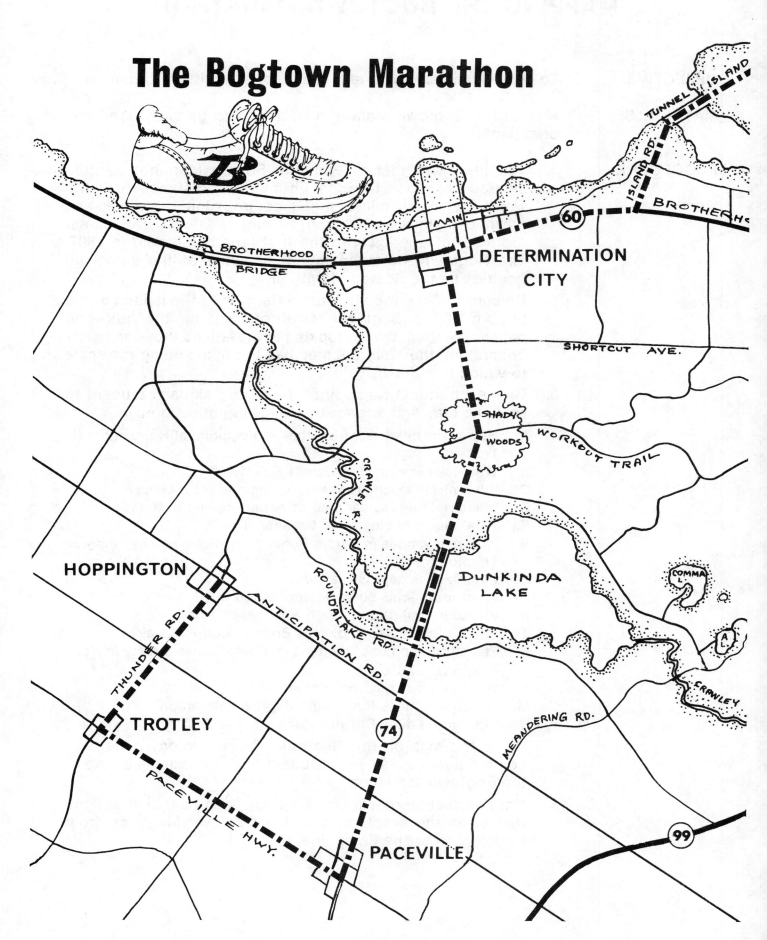

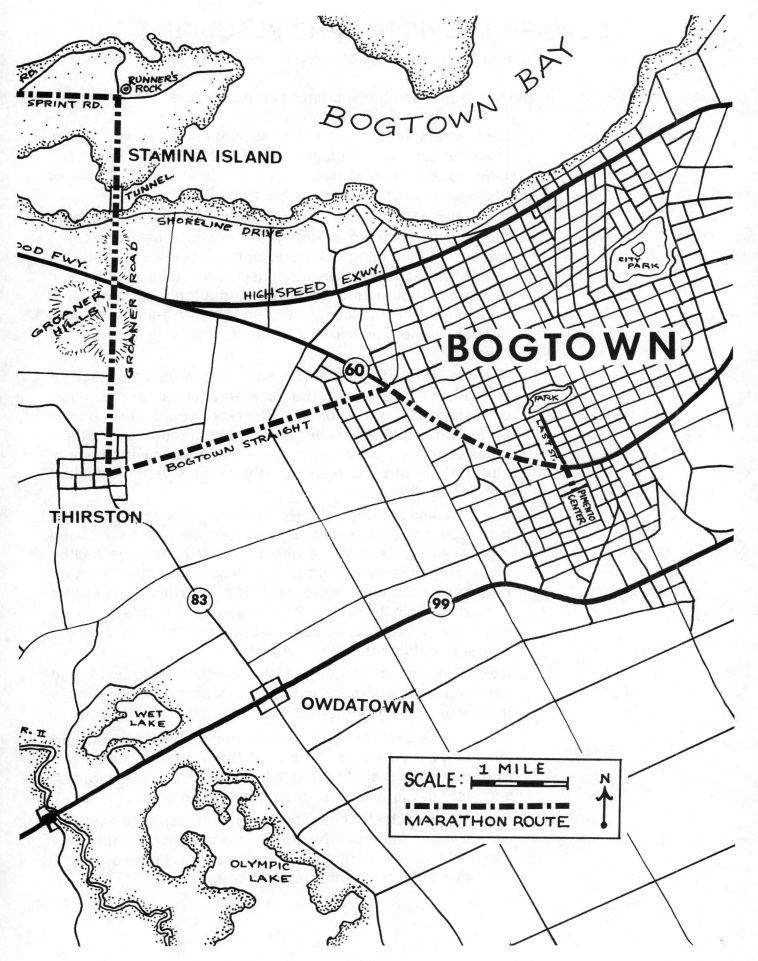

BOGTOWN BAY

STAMINA ISLAND

RUNNER'S ROCK

SPRINT RD.

RD.

TUNNEL

SHORELINE DRIVE

OD FWY.

GROANER HILLS

GROANER ROAD

HIGHSPEED EXWY.

CITY PARK

BOGTOWN

60

PARK

LAST ST.

BOGTOWN STRAIGHT

PIMENTO CENTER

THIRSTON

83

99

R. II

WET LAKE

OWDATOWN

SCALE: 1 MILE

N

MARATHON ROUTE

OLYMPIC LAKE

BEWARE THE NOTE CARD PLAGIARIST

OBJECTIVE: To instruct the student of effective note-taking procedures.

MATERIALS: Markers, Popsicle sticks, bristol board, scissors

PROCEDURE:

1. Discuss plagiarism with the class. Note that the term comes from the Latin word "plagiarius," which means "kidnapper." Literally, a plagiarist is one who steals another's words or ideas and presents them as his own.

2. Warn the class about the various ways one can commit plagiarism either consciously or unconsciously. By being too lazy to take complete notes and too careless to take accurate notes, one can unconsciously take words and phrases without using the proper quotation marks or proper documentation for ideas. Furthermore, by being less than honest, some consciously steal the ideas and words of others.

3. Ask the students to work in pairs and create the face of plagiarism based on the characteristics of laziness, carelessness, and dishonesty. The faces could take the form of masks, cartoon drawings, or abstract designs. These faces could be placed on a bulletin board along with the principles of effective note-taking—the primary defense against accidental plagiarism.

4. Tell the class that there are four uses for note cards. The first is to record direct quotations. Quotation marks must be used around all words that are directly copied from the source material. Ask each student to copy a quotation from a sports biography on a clean note card. The top right-hand corner should contain the name of the source and the page on which the quotation can be found; whereas the top left-hand corner should contain the subject.

5. Next, ask the students to take a clean note card and paraphrase the quotation in their own words. Paraphrasing is the second type of note-taking.

6. Thirdly, ask each student to take the same quotation and summarize it on a clean note card. Summarizing is an effort to briefly note the main idea encompassed in the quote. A summary is vastly shorter than the original quote.

7. Finally, ask each student to take another clean note card and write a comment about the quote. This comment should be a personal reaction to the quote. Be sure to have the students mark this note card with the word "original."

PARAPHRASING SPORTS JOKES

OBJECTIVE: To give the student an opportunity to develop the skill of paraphrasing.

MATERIALS: The list of sports jokes

PROCEDURE:

1. Ask each student to take the following list of sports jokes and paraphrase them by writing them down in words other than already used.

    A. Hundreds of fathers spend thousands of dollars on their sons' higher education and only get a quarterback.

    B. Only in baseball is there a real appreciation of a sacrifice.

    C. Being a good sport is very noble, but you always have to lose to prove it.

    D. The trouble with some golfers is that they stand too close to the ball—after they hit it.

    E. Bending exercises are nothing but an example of stooping to conquer.

    F. The best conditions for skiing call for a lot of white snow and a lot of Blue Cross.

    G. Ducks are Mother Nature's proof that swimming does not always improve the figure.

    H. Basketball, more than any other sport, attracts the highest type of player.

    I. You are over the hill when the most exercise you get is watching televised sports.

    J. It's not the minutes you take at the table that add to your weight—it's the seconds.

    K. A diet is one thing you must stick to through thick and thin.

    L. There are only three things a serious dieter should put in his mouth—a knife, a fork, and a spoon.

2. To further test the skill of paraphrasing, ask the students to select six of the twelve sports jokes and write them in two-line rhymes.

3. Working in pairs, the students could illustrate the jokes via cartooning as a creative extension.

The best conditions for skiing call for a lot of white snow and a lot of Blue Cross.

ON THE OFFENSE

OBJECTIVE: To give students the opportunity to interpret diagrams.

MATERIALS: A large empty room, a chalkboard, chalk, and the diagrams on the next page

PROCEDURE:
1. Draw each of the following diagrams of offensive football formations on the chalkboard:
   A. The single wing
   B. The T
   C. The split T
   D. The winged T
2. Identify the positions by their letter code: E is for the end; LE is left end; RE is right end; T is for tackle; G is for guard; C is for center; QB is for quarterback; WB is for wingback; FB is for fullback; LHB is for left halfback; and RHB is for right halfback.
3. Ask the students to get into two groups of eleven and arrange themselves according to one of the formation diagrams. Students not in a group can act as coaches and assign positions.
4. Next, ask each group to run, one at a time, into the middle of the room, go into a huddle and, at the call of the quarterback, take the field in proper formation.

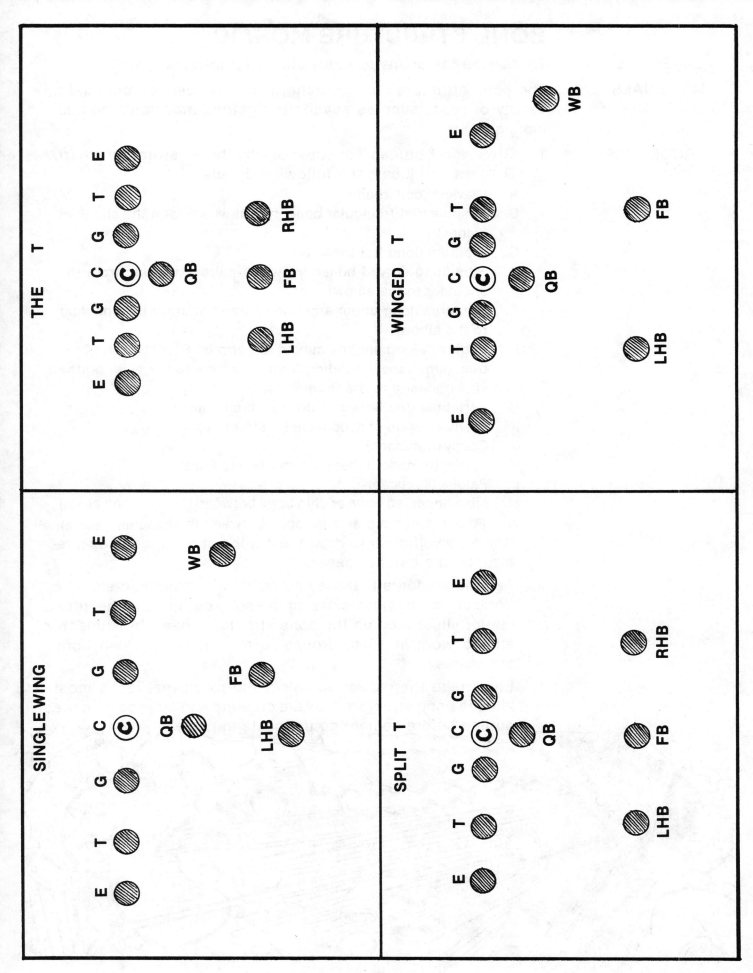

SINGLE WING

THE T

WINGED T

SPLIT T

BONE STRUCTURE MOSAIC

OBJECTIVE: To develop the ability to study charts for information.

MATERIALS: The bone structure chart, butcher paper, rubber cement, and a variety of pasta such as spaghetti, rigatoni, macaroni, mostaccioli, etc.

PROCEDURE:
1. Give each student a copy of the bone structure chart. Discuss and locate the following details:
   A. Clavicle (collarbone)
   B. Scapula (flat triangular bone, two of which form the shoulder blades)
   C. Sternum (long flat breastbone)
   D. Ribs (long curved bones in twelve pairs extending from the shoulder to the elbow)
   E. Humerus (long upper arm bone extending from the shoulder to the elbow)
   F. Radius (a long slightly curved forearm bone)
   G. Ulna (arm bone extending from the elbow to the wrist on the side opposite to the thumb)
   H. Vertebrae (the bones of the spinal column)
   I. Pelvis (a basin-shaped skeletal structure)
   J. Coccyx (tailbone)
   K. Femur (thighbone between pelvis and knee)
   L. Patella (kneecap)
   M. Tibia (inner leg bone or shin bone between the knee and ankle)
   N. Fibula (outer and smaller bone between the knee and ankle)
2. Ask for a volunteer to draw the outline of a human body (life-size) on the butcher paper.
3. Tell the students that they will all have a hand in creating a bone structure mosaic. Using the body outline and the information illustrated on the bone structure chart, the students should work in small groups to create the fourteen bone structures.
4. Encourage the groups to select the pasta that looks most like the bone structure they are creating and arrange it on the outline before cementing the pasta in place.

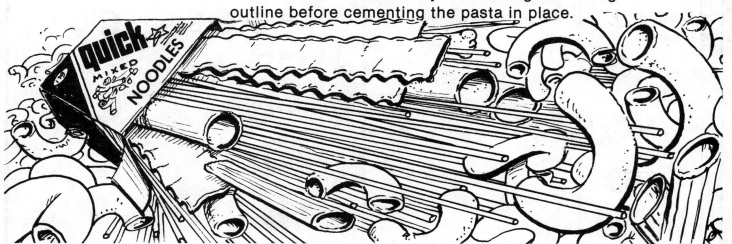

44

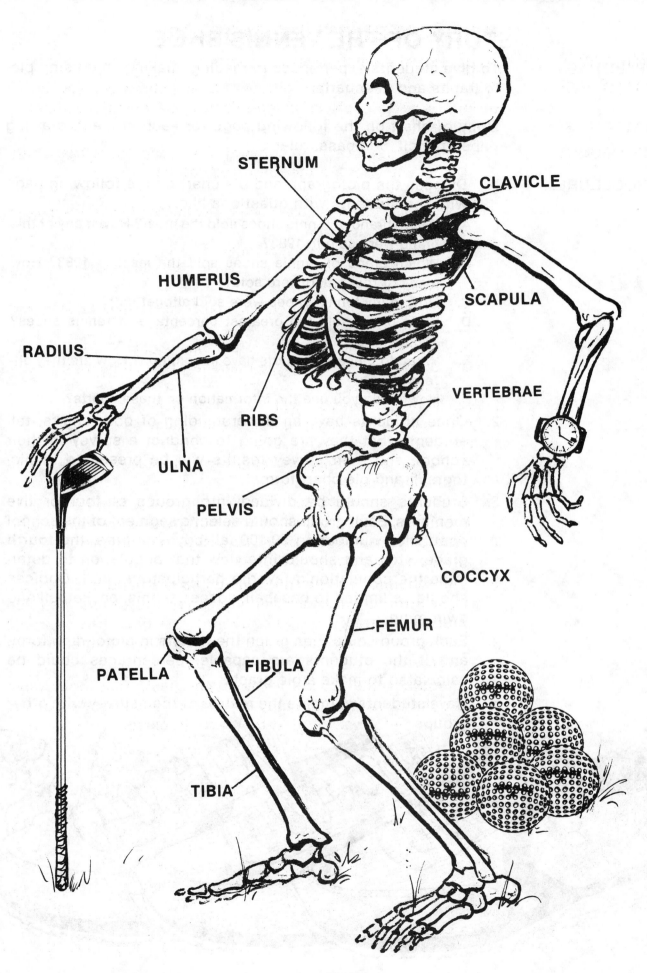

STERNUM

CLAVICLE

HUMERUS

SCAPULA

RADIUS

VERTEBRAE

RIBS

ULNA

PELVIS

COCCYX

FEMUR

PATELLA

FIBULA

TIBIA

STORY OF THE TENNIS SHOE

OBJECTIVE: To give students experiences in reading, making, and using pictographs and pie charts.

MATERIALS: Copy of chart on the following page for each student, drawing paper, pencil, compass, ruler

PROCEDURE:
1. Discuss the pictograph and pie chart on the following page with the students with questions like:
   A. Which brand of tennis shoes sold the most? How many of this brand were sold in 1983?
   B. Which brand of tennis shoes sold the least in 1983? How many of this brand were sold?
   C. How many tennis shoes were sold altogether?
   D. What brand sold the greatest percentage of tennis shoes? The least?
   E. What do these two charts have in common? How are they different?
   F. How could you use the information on these charts?
2. Once students have an understanding of both charts, tell students that they are going to conduct a survey in their school, and their survey results will be presented in pictograph and pie chart format.
3. Students should be divided into groups of four or five members. Each group should select a segment of the school population numbering 50-100 (all boys, all girls, the fourth grade, etc.) and should interview that population to determine the population's favorite participatory sport. Choices should be limited to baseball, soccer, tennis, basketball and swimming.
4. Each group could then graph the results in pictograph form, and if the students are capable, percentages could be calculated to make a pie graph.
5. Have students compare the results of their survey with other groups.

TENNIS SHOE SALES 1983

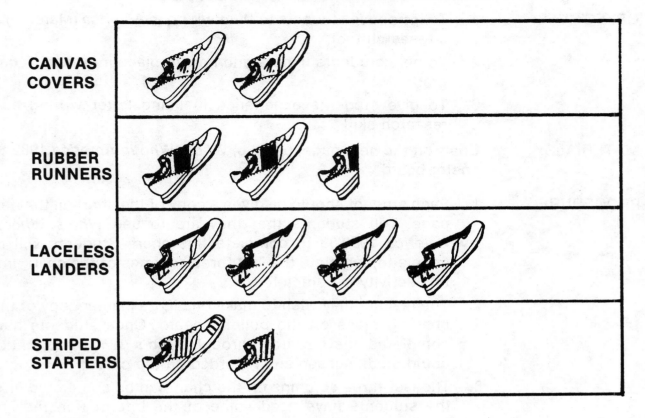

 = 1,000 pair

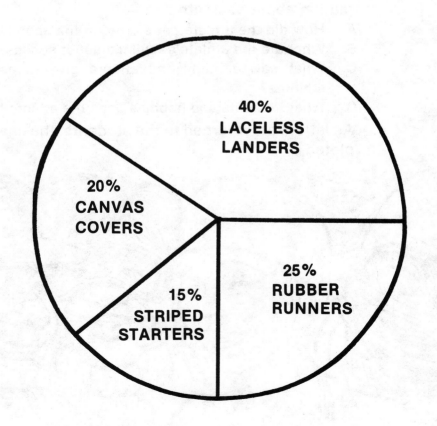

WHO'S WHO IN THE WORLD OF SPORTS

OBJECTIVES:
1. To introduce students to *Who's Who in America* (Marquis) as a research tool.
2. To help students understand how to place information on a graph.
3. To give students experience in using letter writing as a research skill.

MATERIALS:
Chart on the next page, pencils, *Who's Who in America* 1982-83, poster board.

PROCEDURE:
1. Each student should be given a copy of the chart on the next page. Tell students that they are to use *Who's Who in America* 1982-83 to complete this chart. Students will be unable to complete the last three columns of the chart until this activity is completed.

2. The teacher may wish to make one large master copy of this chart to place on the bulletin board. Once students have completed their search through *Who's Who*, information could be discussed and recorded on the chart.

3. The last three columns on the chart can be completed after the students have used some of the information they researched. Each student should be encouraged to write a business letter to any one of the athletes listed in the chart (addresses are available in *Who's Who*). In these letters students should be encouraged to find out additional information about each athlete.
   A. How did the athlete get started in the sport?
   B. What are the athlete's feelings about success?
   C. What advice might the athlete give to aspiring student athletes?
   D. What interests and hobbies does the athlete have?

4. As letters are returned to the students, the chart can be completed.

	Profession	Birthdate	Spouse	Honors earned (any two)	College attended	Degree earned	Address	How started in sport	Feelings about honors earned	Other interests, hobbies
William Walton										
Gordon Howe										
David Lopes										
Paul William Bryant										
Muhammad Ali										
Al Unser										
William Henry Rodgers										
John Pat McEnroe										
Bruce Jenner										
Billie Jean King										

WHAT A RACKET

OBJECTIVE: To give students experiences in reading and using line and bar graphs as research tools.

MATERIALS: Metric ruler, tennis racquet, Ping-Pong paddle, racquetball, racquet, squash racquet, badminton racquet, graph paper for each student, pencils

PROCEDURE:

1. Display racquets for all students to see. Ask students to measure the height of each racquet in centimeters.

2. Explain to students that bar and line graphs are visual aids that display and summarize information (usually comparative information) in grid format. The teacher may wish to demonstrate how bar and line graphs are made by taking a simple class survey of favorite colors and graphing the information on the chalkboard.

3. Tell students that they are to record the comparative heights of the different racquets they measured in two manners: a bar graph and a line graph.

4. Optional: If older students have been introduced to the concepts, the teacher may wish to encourage them to compute things like average, median, and midpoint from information recorded on graphs.

5. When the graphing project has been completed, the teacher may wish to display the graphs on a bulletin board.

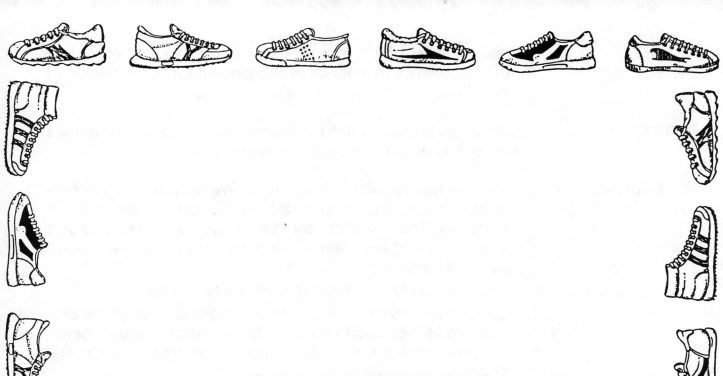

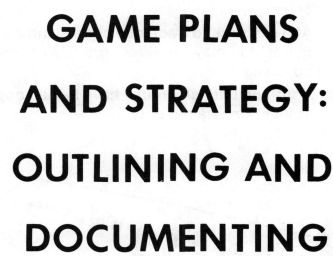

GAME PLANS
AND STRATEGY:
OUTLINING AND
DOCUMENTING

INVENT A SPORT

OBJECTIVE: To offer students experiences in sequencing through creation of a "sport."

MATERIALS: 5 badminton birdies, 5 old tennis shoes, 5 jump ropes, 5 shoe boxes, poster board and magic markers

PROCEDURE:
1. Divide students into five groups. Give each group one badminton birdie, one old tennis shoe, one jump rope, and one shoe box. Tell students that they are going to create a sport using ONLY these items. The sport must, however, incorporate all four items.

2. Allow students 20-30 minutes to create the sport.

3. Once groups have finished, ask each group to write the procedures for the sport on poster board. Remind the students that the procedures and rules must be written in sequential order.

4. Allow groups to trade rule sheets and allow each group to attempt to play another group's game while the class observes.

5. Continue until all groups have had an opportunity to attempt at least one game.

The Game of Bird-Watching
Rules:

1. Each player must use only one watch.
2. The distance between the player and the target bird is ten meters.
3. In turn, each player must try to toss a watch, looping the band over the target bird's body.
4. Ten points are earned for a complete ringing of the bird, five for a beak-loop, th... for a ten centimeter radius ...re the bird stands.

GIVING AN ORDER

OBJECTIVE: To help students use and understand a sequential pattern in research and writing.

MATERIALS: Several copies of sports sections and articles from current newspapers and publications dealing with sports and fitness, one envelope per student, scissors, paper, glue, and poster board, magic markers, drawing paper (optional)

PROCEDURE:

1. Ask students to collect newspaper and magazine articles about sports and fitness. Please alert students that these articles cannot be returned.

2. As students bring articles to school, the teacher should cut each article into separate paragraphs and place all paragraphs from one article into an envelope.

3. When there are enough envelopes for each student in the class, the teacher may wish to review what is involved in sequencing. Remind students that many things have a natural order. Other things are sequenced by time, seasons, aging, etc. Sequencing is simply an ordering of events or ideas.

4. Distribute envelopes to students, and ask each student to glue the paragraphs in his/her envelope on a sheet of paper in sequential order. Discuss the time clues that students used to order their paragraphs.

5. Optional: Students may wish to illustrate cartoons about "How to Play . . . ." The cartoons could then be cut into separate frames and placed in envelopes. Students may enjoy trading envelopes and sequencing others' ideas.

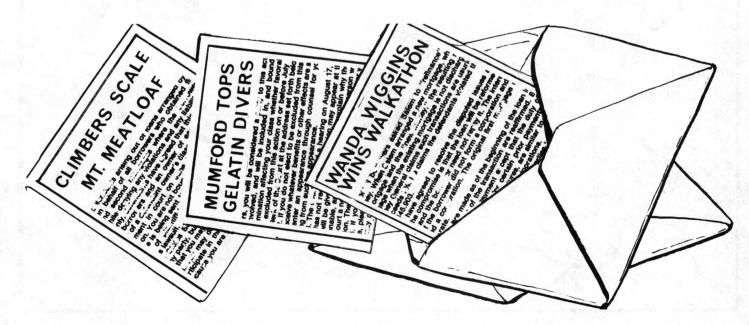

GO FLY A KITE

OBJECTIVE: To introduce students to the format of outlining.

MATERIALS: Paper, pencil, illustration on the next page, several books about kite making and kite flying from the library, markers, and drawing paper

PROCEDURE:

1. After a brief class discussion about kites and kite flying, present the following words to the students. Ask them to put the words into two categories: "Types of Kites" and "Materials Needed to Make a Kite."

Japanese	glider	delta
scissors	yardstick	bird
pencil	diamond	sandpaper
bow	plastic	tape
string	tissue paper	glue
demon	paint	wood

2. Once students have categorized the words, demonstrate the standard outline form on the board.
    I. Types of kites   (main idea)
       A.
       B.
       C.   (subheadings)
       D.
          1.
          2.   (details)
          3.
    II. Materials needed to make a kite

3. You may wish to encourage students to research two facts about each type of kite in order to demonstrate the use of details.

4. As you demonstrate outlining, remind the students:
    A. Major sections are indicated by Roman numerals, subheadings by capital letters, and details are indicated by Arabic numerals.
    B. Where there is an A, there must be a B, where there is a 1, there must be a 2, etc.
    C. Outlines serve as organizational frameworks for most research.
    D. The first word in main ideas and subheadings is always capitalized.

5. Explain to students that a sentence outline incorporates the same format; however, main ideas and subheadings will be written in complete sentences.

6. Give each student a copy of the paragraph that is on the next page, and with your guidance, ask students to write brief sentence outlines from the information in that paragraph.

7. Ask students to use books about kite flying to write brief outlines about either the "History of Kite Flying" or "How to Make a Kite."

8. Optional: The teacher may wish to have students either draw pictures of the kites mentioned in "Procedure #1," or make kites to be displayed in the room.

KITE FLYING TECHNIQUES

Kite flying is a delightful activity for people of all ages; however, successful kite flying requires mastery of certain techniques. The first consideration is to find a perfect location for flying your kite. Large open areas which do not have traffic, trees, or power lines are perfect. Also, a place near a large body of water is recommended because light winds from the water are helpful. Wind condition is the second consideration when flying your kite. Steady winds between four and fifteen miles per hour are ideal. Winds blowing across the earth's surface are better than breezes that will lift and lower your kite in a moment. Contrary to popular opinion, a person does not have to run in order to launch a kite. Getting it into the air, the last consideration, can be accomplished by holding the kite in the air with your back toward the wind. As you feel a breeze, allow the kite to lift making certain to keep the string taut. No wonder kite flying appeals to so many people.

There is not a kite-flying technique that is complete without a discussion of safety precautions. Kites should never be launched near power lines. If your kite happens to get caught in a power line, NEVER remove it yourself. Let your power company handle the problem. Secondly, never fly a kite in the rain as electricity builds up in the clouds and can cause shock. Never fly kites near streets or roadways. Avoid using kites or kite strings that have wire or metal in them. Lastly, you might wish to wear gloves to protect your hands when flying a kite. When flying a kite, your enjoyment can depend upon your safety precautions.

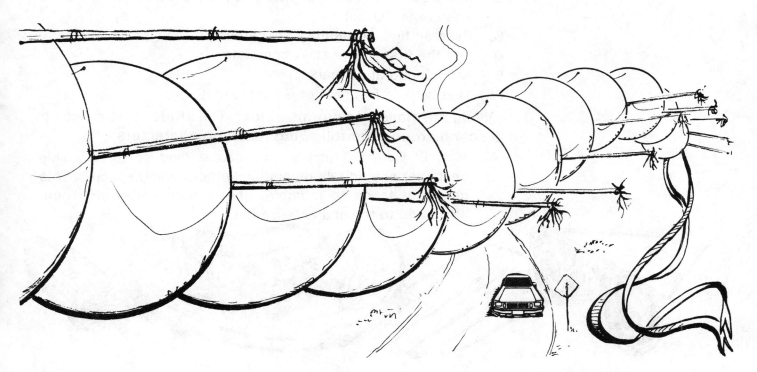

RESEARCH CHARACTERS

OBJECTIVE: To become familiar with words and abbreviations used in research.

MATERIALS: Sunglasses, ladies' white gloves, big flowery hat, chewing gum and key list of reference words

PROCEDURE:
1. Give the students the following key list of research terms and abbreviations:
   A. bib. stands for "bibliography"
   B. biog. stands for "biography"
   C. C stands for "copyright"
   D. ch. stands for "chapter"
   E. comp. stands for "compiled by"
   F. ed. stands for "edited by"
   G. et al. stands for "and others"
   H. etc. stands for "and so forth"
   I. e.g. stands for "for example"
   J. fig. stands for "figure"
   K. ibid. stands for "in the same place"
   L. ms. stands for "manuscript"
   M. N.B. or Nota Bene stands for "take notice"
   N. pseud. stands for "pseudonym"
   O. pub. stands for "publisher"
   P. vol. stands for "volume"

2. Ask the students to untangle the following sentences of research talk using the key list:
   A. To locate the pub. and ed. check the bib. Ibid. for the vol. and chap.
   B. Many authors prefer to write under a pseud. (e.g., Dr. Seuss and Lewis Carroll).
   C. Read all figs. in the ms. very carefully.
   D. List the first author et al. completely.
   E. N.B. all quotation marks.
   F. That book is by Jennifer Gillespie et al.

3. Divide the class into groups of four. Tell students to make up a scene around the following research characters:
   A. Mrs. Et Cetera (Literally this means "and so forth.") This character should talk on and on without being specific. This character tends to mumble. She is flighty. Chewing gum could add to the characterization.

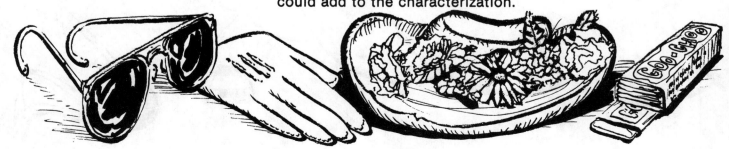

B. Mr. Pseud. (Literally a pseudonym is a disguise.) This character should talk in a hushed voice and use code words. Costume piece could be dark glasses.

C. Miss Exempli Gratia. (Literally this means "for example.") This character is very specific in her language. This character is a perfectionist. She is very neat. Costume piece could be white gloves.

D. Ms. Nota Bene. (Literally this means "take notice.") This character is very loud and boisterous. This character has a very large ego. She is conceited and pushy. Costume piece could be a big flowery hat.

Environments for the scene could be a sports talk show on television, a sporting goods store, a locker room, or a grandstand at a sporting event. Encourage each student to move and talk as the character would move and talk. Props and costume pieces can be used.

4. Share the scenes with the whole class by showing them one at a time.

THE BICYCLE CHRONICLES

OBJECTIVE: To further the understanding of outlining based on a chronological organization.

MATERIALS: Paper and pencils

PROCEDURE:
1. Ask each student to think back to his first tricycle.
   A. What color was your first tricycle?
   B. At what age did you get your first tricycle?
   C. What did you think of it?
   D. Did it have any particular characteristics such as a bell or a horn?
   E. Did it have a basket or a license plate?
   F. How long did the tricycle last?
   G. Did you ever use the tricycle for things other than riding?

2. Tell the students that each is going to write a history of the bicycle in his/her life. Direct them to do research for the next day's work by engaging in the following activities:
   A. Look at your baby books to see what your first bike looked like.
   B. Look at family albums to trace the progression of bikes from tricycles to bicycles to ten-speeds to dirt bikes to mini bikes.
   C. Ask parents about the things that happened to you and your bike such as accidents and bike races.

3. At the next class, ask the students to organize their outlines chronologically. Begin with the information concerning the first tricycle and proceed through the years to the information on the last or current bike.

4. When the outlines have been completed with both statements and support materials, the students are ready to write *The Bicycle Chronicles.*

OUTLINING BIKE SAFETY

OBJECTIVE: To study the topical organization of outlining.

MATERIALS: Props from home as needed for the pantomimes and materials to construct four life-size cardboard bicycles (markers, glue, bristol board, scissors) and the outline on the following page to be used on overhead projector

PROCEDURE:
1. Ask each student to research and write an outline on bicycle safety using the following topical organization:
   A. Keep the bike in good running condition.
   B. Wear the proper clothing for biking.
   C. Follow the rules of road safety.
   D. Anticipate dangers.
2. Divide the class into four groups. Assign one topic of the outline to each group. Ask group members to pool their research and come up with three to five things the biker should do that elaborates the topic. These three to five "do's" should be worked into a mime:
   A. Group A could demonstrate keeping the bike in good running condition by miming such actions as oiling the bike, tightening the handlebars, checking the brakes, and adjusting the seat.
   B. Group B could demonstrate wearing proper clothing by selecting "bright" colors, putting on headgear and helmets, taking off hooded jackets that obstruct vision, and tying down pant legs so they will not get caught in the chain set.
   C. Group C could demonstrate proper road safety by miming riding against traffic, using proper hand signals, obeying traffic signs, and not putting more than one rider on a bicycle.
   D. Group D could demonstrate how to anticipate dangers such as looking ahead for problems on the road surface, being aware of conjested intersections, noticing that fog is starting to settle in, and watching out for intruding dogs.
3. Ask each group to design a life-size cardboard cutout of a bicycle to use in the mimes by following the outline on the next page.
4. Share the pantomimes.

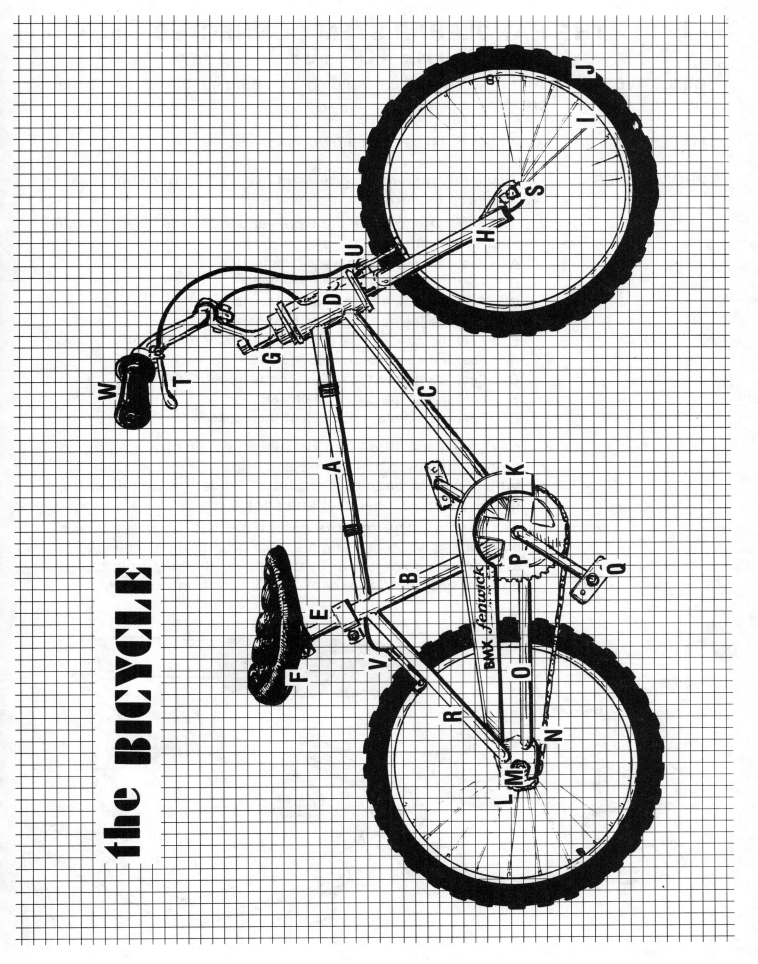

the BICYCLE

THE HANDLEBAR STEM CONNECTED
TO THE TOP TUBE

OBJECTIVE: To further the understanding of outlining based on spatial organization.

MATERIALS: A number of bikes owned by class members

PROCEDURES:
1. Place the students in groups of five. Each group should have a bike to explore via touch and sight.
2. Ask students to close their eyes and touch the bike from one end to the other.
    A. Feel the rubber or plastic handlegrips.
    B. Feel the coldness of the handlebars.
    C. Feel the shape of the handlebar stem.
    D. Feel the leather or plastic seat or saddle.
    E. Feel the curve of the chrome fenders or mudguards.
    F. Feel the shape of the mudguards.
    G. Feel the rubber tires with their textured surface.
    H. Feel the shape of the chain set.
    I. Feel the slender coolness of the spokes.
3. Next, ask each student to visually study the bike from top to bottom including handlebars and grips, handlebar stem, top tube, seat or saddle, seat tube, fenders and reflectors, wheels, spokes, chain set and pedals.
4. Ask each student to write an outline that describes how a bike looks and feels using a spatial organization. The spatial relation can come about by describing the bike from top to bottom, bottom to top, back to front, or front to back.

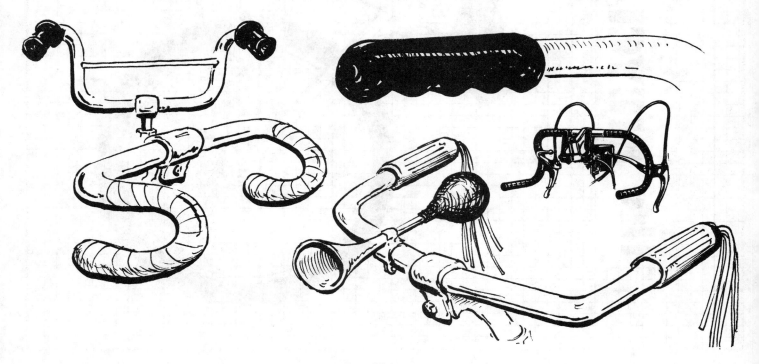

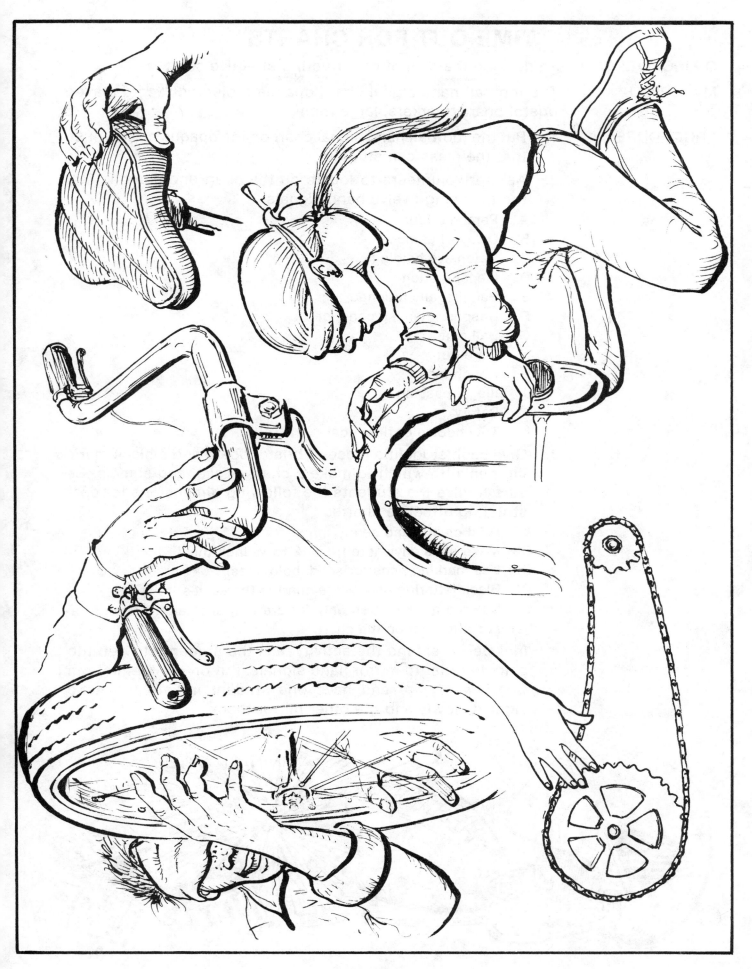

TIME OUT FOR CHARTS

OBJECTIVE: To develop the skill of constructing effective charts.

MATERIALS: The football hand signal chart, opaque projector, record player, bristol board, markers, large room

PROCEDURE:
1. Put the football hand signal chart on the opaque projector so that the class can study it.

2. Ask for volunteers to locate on the chart and demonstrate the following twelve hand signals:
   A. Personal foul
   B. Delay of game
   C. Defensive holding
   D. Illegal motion
   E. Ball illegally touched
   F. Unsportsmanlike conduct
   G. Ball dead
   H. Time out
   I. Roughness
   J. Illegal passing
   K. Safety
   L. Touchdown or field goal

3. Give each student a piece of bristol board and a black marking pen with which to make a chart of six hand signals. Be sure to give the students the following dimensions for constructing effective charts:
   A. Print clearly and neatly.
   B. Make lines anywhere from ¼ to ½ inch thick.
   C. Use marking pens for solid, bold lines.
   D. Black lettering on a white chart is the easiest to read.
   E. Use red marking pen only for drawing special attention to a specific item on the chart.

4. In order to extend the activity, ask the students to get into pairs in order to mirror hand signals. Put on the theme from *Chariots of Fire* and have one student initiate the hand signals slowly and the other mirror them.

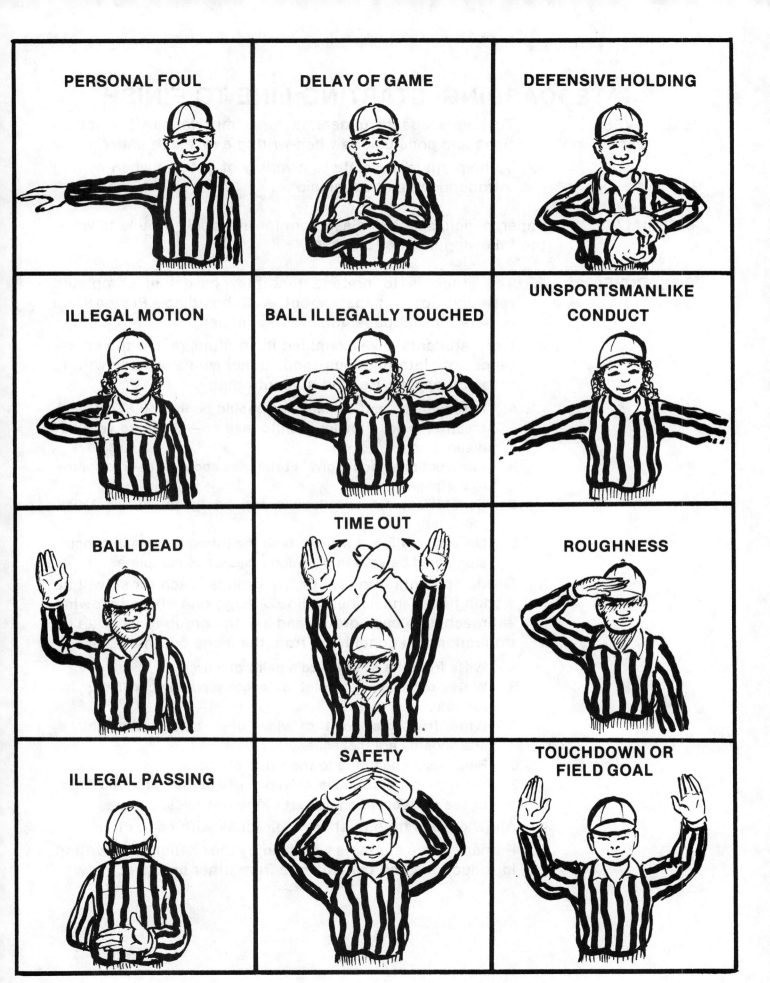

PERSONAL FOUL

DELAY OF GAME

DEFENSIVE HOLDING

ILLEGAL MOTION

BALL ILLEGALLY TOUCHED

UNSPORTSMANLIKE CONDUCT

BALL DEAD

TIME OUT

ROUGHNESS

ILLEGAL PASSING

SAFETY

TOUCHDOWN OR FIELD GOAL

SKATEBOARDING: STARTING LINE TO FINISH

OBJECTIVES:
1. To help students understand the importance of introductions and conclusions when writing a research paper.
2. To help students relate to a variety of options when writing introductions and conclusions.

MATERIALS:
Paper, pencil, space in classroom for five or six groups to work, the following illustration page

PROCEDURE:
1. Tell students to pretend that they have just completed research for a paper about skateboarding. Present the outline for that paper (on the next page).
2. Once students have examined the outline, review the importance of introductions and conclusions when writing research papers. Remind students that:
    A. Introductions and conclusions should be INTERESTING and creative, make a reader wish to read on—appeal to your audience.
    B. Introductions should give a brief idea about what is to follow in the paper.
    C. Conclusions tie up all ends and briefly review what has preceded.
    D. Once an outline is written, both the introduction and conclusion could be written provided research is complete.
3. Divide students into four or five groups. Each group will be working from the same outline. Assign one of the following approaches to each group, and ask the group to write an introduction and conclusion from the same outline:
    A. Write from the skateboard's point of view.
    B. Write from the viewpoint of a conservation-conscious individual.
    C. Write from the point of view of a person who thinks skateboards are menaces.
    D. Relate skateboarding to the world of sports.
    E. Write the paper from the viewpoint of a person who would like to see skateboarding as part of the Olympics.
4. Allow groups time to share their ideas with each other.
5. Perhaps some students would enjoy the challenge of writing introductions and conclusions from other points of view.

SKATEBOARDING

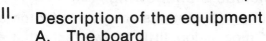

I. History of skateboarding
  A. The wheel as a forerunner
  B. The scooter as a forerunner
  C. 1962—became a sport
  D. Current status of the sport

II. Description of the equipment
  A. The board
    1. Other names
    2. Composition
    3. Nomenclature
  B. The truck
  C. The wheels
    1. Materials used
    2. Types of bearings
    3. Maintenance

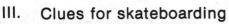

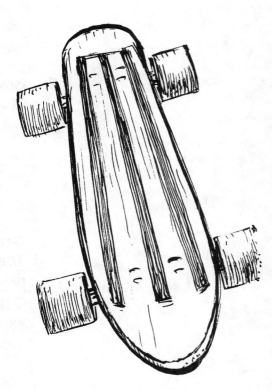

III. Clues for skateboarding
  A. Clothing for the sport
  B. Where to skateboard
  C. How to inspect board
  D. When to skateboard

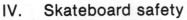

IV. Skateboard safety
  A. How to fall
  B. How to learn
  C. Four basic rules

V. Methods of riding
  A. Sitting
  B. Standing
  C. Beginning
  D. Stopping
  E. Turning
  F. Tricks
    1. Wheelie
    2. Hang ten
    3. Kick-turn

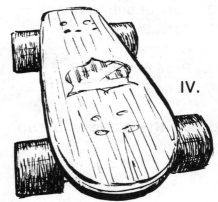

IV. Laws governing sport
  A. Outlawed in some states
  B. Laws for your city

"FOOTING" THE FOOTNOTE

OBJECTIVE: To help students understand the function and form of footnoting.

MATERIALS: Approximately 14 copies of the "foot" stencil on the next page, a large open area in which students can move freely, marker, stopwatch (optional)

PROCEDURE:
1. Review the purposes of footnotes with the students. Be sure to include the following:
   A. Direct quotations are always footnoted.
   B. On occasion, little known facts that are cited are footnoted.
   C. It is a good idea to footnote controversial statements.
   D. A writer usually uses another person's statement when that statement supports the author's view.
   E. Footnotes are used not only to avoid plagiarism, but also to help interested readers do further research and investigation.

2. Review the following standard footnote forms with the students:
   A. Book:
      [1]Author, <u>Book Title</u> (Place of publication: publisher, date of publication), page number.
   B. Magazine article:
      [2]Author, "Article Title," <u>Magazine</u>, volume number (Date), page number.

   Depending upon the age and ability level of your students, *The MLA Style Sheet* or many English texts are good reference sources for additional information on footnotes.

3. Cut out approximately 28 "feet" and on each "foot" write a word or expression. (make two sets).

1. Indent	9. Colon
2. Footnote number	10. Publisher
3. Author	11. Comma
4. Comma	12. Date of publication
5. Title	13. Parenthesis
6. Underline	14. Comma
7. Parenthesis	15. Page number
8. Place of publication	16. Period

4. Shuffle each set of "feet," and divide the class into two groups. Select a leader for each group.

5. Give each leader one set of "feet," and tell everyone they are about to become footnotes. The leader is to assign each group member a "foot," and these feet must arrange themselves in standard footnote form.

6. Time group members as they arrange themselves. Repeat the exercise until all interested students have a chance to lead.

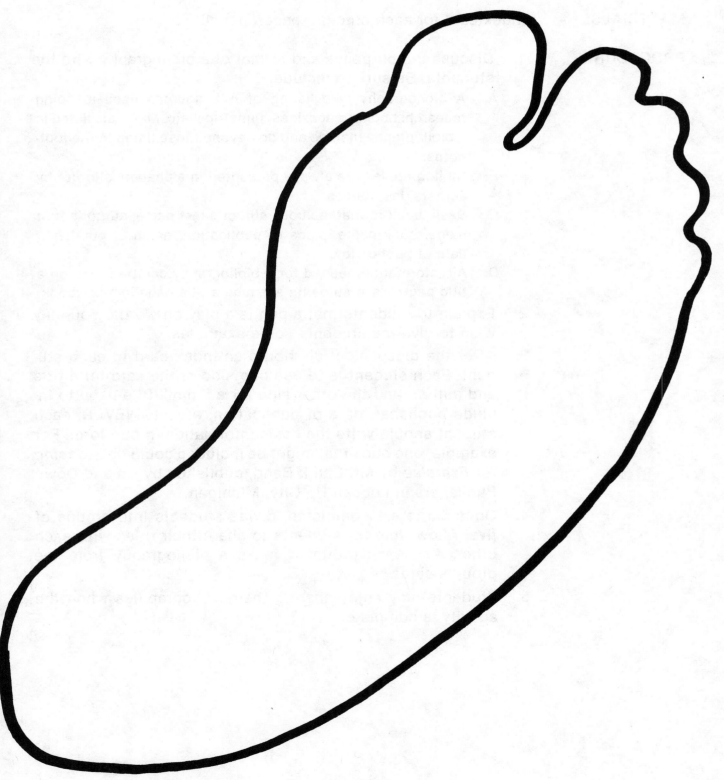

PUNNING THE BIBLIOGRAPHY

OBJECTIVES: 1. To help students understand how to present a bibliography in a research paper.
2. To help students understand the format and function of a bibliography in research.

MATERIALS: Index card for each student, paper, pencil

PROCEDURE: 1. Discuss the purposes and format of a bibliography with the students. Be sure to include:
A. A bibliography is a listing of ALL sources used in doing research: books, magazines, filmstrips, etc. Materials listed in a bibliography include and go beyond those listed in the footnotes.
B. Bibliographies are always presented in alphabetical order by authors' last names.
C. Basic book format includes author's last name, author's first name, book name, place of publication, name of publisher, date of publication.
D. All information needed for a bibliography can be found on a title page. Have students examine a title page in a textbook.
2. Explain to students that a pun is a play on words. You may wish to give the students some examples.
3. After the discussion, distribute an index card to each student. Each student is to use one side of the card for a title and author, and the other side for a "mini" title page to include publisher, date of publication, etc. HOWEVER, each student should write the basic information in pun form. For example, one book that might be included could be *Stooping for Exercise* by Mr. Can I. Bend, published by Up and Down Publishers in Loosen Up City, Michigan.
4. Once cards are completed, divide students into groups of five. Allow time for students to share their titles with each other. Ask each group to make a bibliography from the group's cards.
5. Students may enjoy sharing their bibliographies when the activity is complete.

STOOPING FOR EXERCISE

1983 EDITION

by

CAN I. BEND

UP AND DOWN PUBLISHERS

Loosen Up City, Michigan

GIVE ME EVIDENCE!

OBJECTIVE: To study the four main categories of evidence used to document statements.

MATERIALS: Picture on illustration page

PROCEDURE:

1. Explain to the students that evidence is used to give support to the statements made within the body of the paper or speech. Evidence can document what you say. This "support material" can be identified by the following categories:

   A. **Quotations**
   Quotations are powerful, especially if they are by experts in the field because they back statements up with credibility.

   B. **Statistics**
   Statistics including ratios, percentages, and figures are useful in offering concrete proof that statements are true.

   C. **Stories**
   Stories and narratives such as anecdotes, parables, fables, and personal experiences can often elaborate on statements while also supporting them.

   D. **Examples**
   Examples are useful in clarifying statements because they support by giving specific instances.

2. Give each student a copy of the illustration. Ask each student to locate examples, stories, quotations, or statistics to support the following statements. Each student should write down the answers to the following ten questions by finding support material in the picture.

   A. Tennis shoes are not as expensive as bowling shoes. (Find an example.)
   B. The store policy is very humorous. (Find a quotation.)
   C. Small children can get hurt if unattended in a sporting goods store. (Find a story.)
   D. There were more males in the sporting goods store at 10:00 a.m. than females. (Find a statistic.)
   E. The store employees contributed more generously in 1984 than in 1983 to the United Fund Drive. (Find a statistic.)
   F. Imported goods are not selling well this year. (Find a quote.)

G. Exercise bikes are very popular this year. (Find a story.)
H. There are some wonderful bargains at the sporting goods store. (Find an example.)
I. Professional tennis players prefer aluminum rackets. (Find a quotation.)
J. Some salespeople are bored with their jobs. (Find an example.)

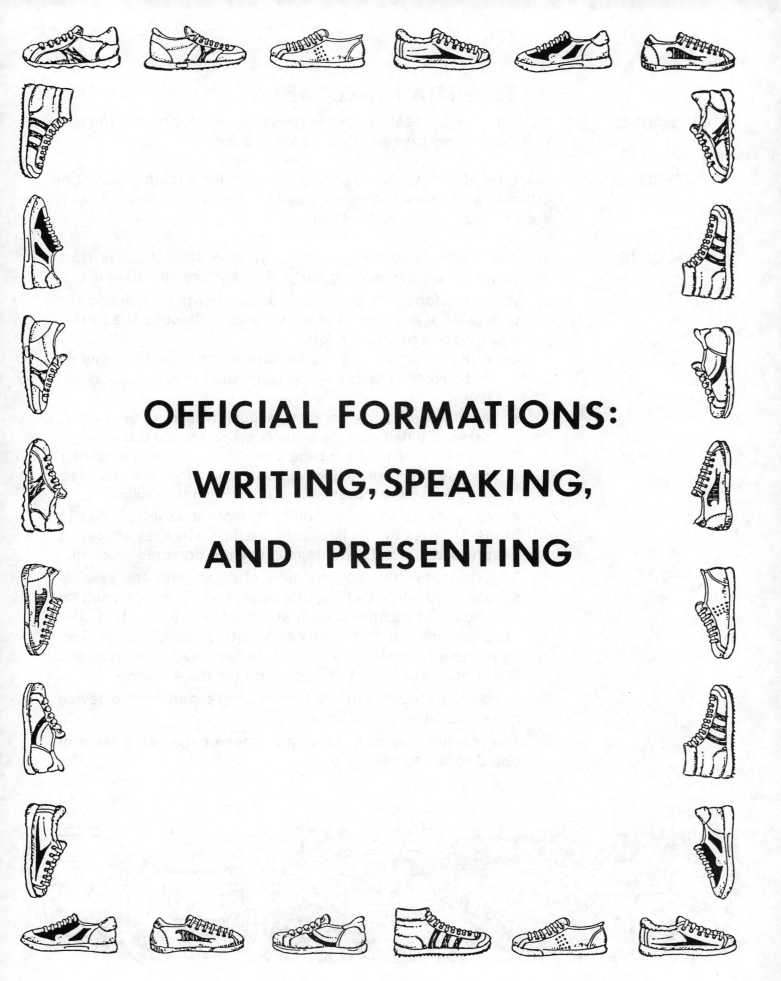

OFFICIAL FORMATIONS:
WRITING, SPEAKING,
AND PRESENTING

THE TRAINING TABLE

OBJECTIVE: To introduce students to the purpose and function of a title and title page when presenting a research paper.

MATERIALS: Samples of various types of health foods for a tasting party (include yogurt, honey, carob, granola, raisins, sunflower seeds, etc.), paper, pencil, and markers

PROCEDURE:

1. Ask students to bring various types of health foods from home for a class tasting party. Be aware of any allergies.

2. While the foods are displayed, ask students to examine the title page of any one of their textbooks. Discuss the format and purpose of a title page:
   A. A title page includes the full title of the book, full name of author(s), the publishing company, and the place of publication.
   B. Any research paper for class should include a title, author, date submitted, and the name or section of the class.
   C. The title of reports and papers should not only be interesting enough to encourage the readers to begin the paper, but also should give the reader an idea about what is to follow.

3. Allow students the opportunity to taste a variety of health foods. Discuss things like taste, texture, why they are called health foods, etc. (Students may wish to do some research.)

4. Tell students that they are now charged with the responsibility of designing a title, title page, and cover (optional) for a book about health foods that includes five chapters. The chapters are titled: "What Are Health Foods," "Why Consume Health Foods?" "101 Favorite Recipes," "Myths About Nutrition," and "Health Food Menu for the Athlete."

5. Encourage students to use their tasting experience to devise a creative title for the book.

6. The teacher may wish to display these pages on a bulletin board for all to see.

WHY JOHNNY CAN'T BAT

OBJECTIVE: To help students learn to combine sentences in various manners in order to vary sentence structure in writing.

MATERIALS: Paper, pencil, copy of illustration on next two pages for each student

PROCEDURE:

1. Distribute a copy of the illustration to each student. Allow time for class to discuss and enjoy the picture. During a class discussion, the teacher should call attention to things in the picture like facial expression, body language and other illustrations of nonverbal communication.

2. Review sentence structure with the students beginning with the basic Noun-Verb-Noun sentence. Ask the students to give you an example of this type of sentence, and encourage students to help you embellish the sentence with phrases, clauses, adjectives, etc. Tell students that sentences can be expanded in many ways. Three of these methods are:

   A. Use of adjectives
   B. Use of conjunctions: *and, for,* and *but*
   C. Use of relative pronouns: *whose, who, whom, which,* and *that.*

3. Remind students that variety in sentences is often what distinguishes good writing from poor.

4. Once students understand the three types of sentence expansion techniques, divide the class into five or six groups. Ask each group to write ten simple sentences (N-V-N pattern) on a sheet of paper. Each sentence should be about the picture on the illustration page.

5. When the sentences are complete, ask groups to trade sentence cards. Each group must then use the ten simple sentences, and convert them into THREE logical sentences using each expansion technique at least once.

6. Allow time for students to share their sentences with the class.

READING THE UMPIRE

OBJECTIVE: To introduce students to the idiom and its uses in written and verbal communication.

MATERIALS: A large area in the classroom where students can move freely, paper, pencil, and stopwatch (optional)

PROCEDURE:

1. Explain to students that many people must interpret clues and signals in order to function. For example, newscasters must be able to "read" umpires' signals. Players must be able to read coaches' signals. We must be able to interpret signals and clues when we read and write. Signals and clues in written and spoken language are called figurative language. One type of figurative language is called the idiom. An idiom is a group of words, peculiar to a certain language, which cannot always be translated literally.

2. Discuss some examples with the students. For example, we speak of "putting on a thinking cap" when we are encouraging someone to concentrate, or we speak of "thumbs up" to show approval.

3. When the students understand the concept, write each idiom listed below on a separate sheet of paper. Place all papers in a box, and divide students into two teams for charades. Each student will be an "umpire," and select one idiom from the box to charade for the class. The teacher may wish to time the umpires.

4. Once the idiom has been charaded, the teacher may wish to ask the "umpire" to explain the following:
   A. Hitting the nail on the head
   B. Being in hot water
   C. You are off your rocker
   D. Making heads or tails
   E. Sitting on top of the world
   F. Hitting the ceiling
   G. Eating your heart out
   H. Turning over a new leaf
   I. Pulling my leg
   J. Walking on thin ice
   K. Blowing your top
   L. Beating around the bush
   M. Putting a feather in your cap
   N. Talking to the wall
   O. It's money in the bank
   P. There's a bee in your bonnet
   Q. Ants in your pants
   R. The writing is on the wall

SPORTS BEE

OBJECTIVE: To introduce various forms of figurative language to the children.

MATERIALS: List of sentences for teacher use (below), enough classroom space for students to line up in spelling bee format

PROCEDURE:
1. Discuss figurative language and its function with the students. Be sure to include:
   A. Similes—comparisons using words "as" or "like" (bright as gold)
   B. Metaphors—comparison in which a person or thing is given the name of something else (boy is a fox)
   C. Personification—giving something nonhuman human characteristics (ball runs across the field)
   D. Onomatopoeia—words for sounds (bow-wow)
   E. Alliteration—a group of words all having the same beginning sound (six silly sailors)
   F. Hyperbole—exaggeration used for effect

2. Once students have an understanding of the concepts, divide the room in half and have students line up in spelling bee formation.

3. Read the following sentences for students, repeating the underlined phrase, and ask students to identify the figurative language being used. The student answer will be one of the five words presented in number 1.
   A. The lightweight fighter lost so much weight, he looked *as thin as a rail.* (simile)
   B. *Polly Peters positively played Ping-Pong.* (alliteration)
   C. When the pitcher finished nine innings, he was *hungry enough to eat a horse.* (hyperbole)
   D. The hockey player lost his control when the puck *ran across the ice.* (personification)
   E. The *snow on the ski slope was powdered sugar.* (metaphor)
   F. *Crack went the bat* as the pitcher hit a home run. (onomatopoeia)
   G. The ice in the arena was *as smooth as glass* before the hockey game. (simile)
   H. The coach was *as upset as a hungry lion* when his team lost the game. (hyperbole or simile)
   I. *Freddy French fired five fabulous free throws.* (alliteration)

84

J. The *snowmobile was a rocket* in the newly fallen snow. (metaphor)

K. The *kite drank the wind* and soared through the sky. (personification)

L. The *running shoes danced* as the runner neared the finish line. (personification)

M. The golf balls were *piled like mountains* after the tournament. (hyperbole or simile)

N. The *stadium was as clean as a whistle* when the season began. (simile)

O. *Bang went the gun* as the race started. (onomatopoeia)

P. *Spotlighting several special sports shows seems significant* for TV. (alliteration)

Q. The *water was a glove* that enveloped the swimmer's body. (metaphor)

R. As the players collided during the tackle, the helmets *went crash.* (onomatopoeia)

S. The *trophy glistened like gold* in the sun during the awards ceremony. (simile)

T. After the marathon, the runner was *thirsty enough to drink the ocean.* (hyperbole)

U. *Happy Harry handles handsprings horribly.* (alliteration)

V. The *golf ball walked gently* into the ninth hole. (personification)

W. In planning their strategy, the *football team was foxy.* (metaphor)

X. The *horses neighed loudly* as they approached the starting gate. (onomatopoeia)

Y. The team *members remained as cool as cucumbers* when they lost the game. (simile)

IN OTHER WORDS

OBJECTIVE: Experience in selecting precise words via the use of a thesaurus.

MATERIALS: Copies of proverbs on the next page for each student, pencils, five or ten copies of any thesaurus, five pieces of poster board, markers

PROCEDURE:

1. Introduce students to the thesaurus and demonstrate its uses. Be sure to remind students that:
   A. A thesaurus is helpful when you wish to locate a precise word and hope to avoid repetition when writing.
   B. Most copies of a thesaurus include synonyms, antonyms, parts of speech, and sometimes colloquialisms.
   C. A thesaurus is used like a dictionary.
2. Once students have a basic understanding of the thesaurus, divide the class into five groups making certain each group has at least one thesaurus, and each student has a copy of the proverbs on the next page.
3. Ask each group to rewrite the proverbs by using the thesaurus. Once the proverbs have been rewritten, allow time for groups to share their paraphrased proverbs with each other.
4. Tell the groups that they are to become advertising agencies. Each group must select one proverb and use it to market any sports or fitness item. (For example, "Look before you leap" might be used to sell tennis shoes, or "Too many cooks . . ." might be used to market a health food.)
5. The group must then use the proverb, create the product (or sell an existing product), and make a poster advertising that item. These posters could be displayed in the room.

RALPH'S ILLUSTRATED
THESAURUS

A. Haste makes waste.
B. Silence is golden.
C. Look before you leap.
D. Nice guys finish last.
E. Honesty is the best policy.
F. Waste not, want not.
G. A penny saved is a penny earned.
H. Too many cooks spoil the broth.
I. Do unto others as you would have others do unto you.
J. Better to be safe than sorry.

BASEBALL GREATS FROM A TO Z

OBJECTIVE: To establish the practice of diaphragmatic breathing.

MATERIALS: Stopwatch and the list of baseball greats

PROCEDURE:

1. Tell the class that the best breath support for speaking comes from diaphragmatic breathing. In order to locate the diaphragmatic muscle, ask students to bend over as if they were going to pick a ball up off the ground. While students are bent over, ask them to concentrate on the tug they feel that is around their waists. Tell them that is the diaphragmatic muscle. Ask them to exhale and notice how the tug disappears. Repeat this exercise several times until everyone can "feel" the muscle.

2. Next, ask students to stand up straight and again take a deep breath. This time they will have to consciously breathe from the diaphragm. If they put their hands on their waists they should feel their waistlines increase when they inhale and decrease when they exhale. This is an external way they can tell if they are breathing from the diaphragm. This may take several attempts before it is successful. An image of a balloon can help greatly. Tell the students that when they inhale they are filling the balloon around their waists and when they exhale they are deflating the balloon.

3. Ask the students to practice short quick diaphragmatic breathing by "panting" (quick successions of inhales and exhales) as if they had just finished running the bases for a home run.

4. Next, ask the students to inhale and say the word "Go" on the exhale. Again the inhale and exhale will be quick. the whole class can participate vocally by repeating "Go! Go! Go! Go!" (Remind them that each "Go" requires a separate inhale and exhale.)

5. The class should now vocalize a *sustained* tone on one breath stream. Ask them to inhale and phonate "Go," but this time sustain the word as long as they can by economically using the exhalation. In other words, do not let the air out all at once but rather in a steady slow stream. You can use a stopwatch to see how many seconds each class member can sustain the tone.

6. Distribute a copy of the "Baseball Greats from A to Z" to each class member. A contest could take place to see who can get the farthest down the list on just one inhalation-exhalation.

Baseball Greats from A to Z

Hank *A*aron
Yogi *B*erra
Roy *C*ampanella
Joe *Di*Maggio
Johnny *E*vers
Carleton *F*isk
Lou *G*ehrig
Rogers *H*ornsby
Monte *I*rvin
Reggie *J*ackson
Al *K*aline
Bob *L*emon
Mickey *M*antle
Don *N*ewcombe
Red *O*rmsby
Tony *P*erez
John *Q*uinn
Babe *R*uth
Willie *S*targell
Mike *T*orrez
Bob *U*ecker
Fernando *V*alenzuela
Ted *W*illiams
X
Cy *Y*oung
Heine *Z*immerman

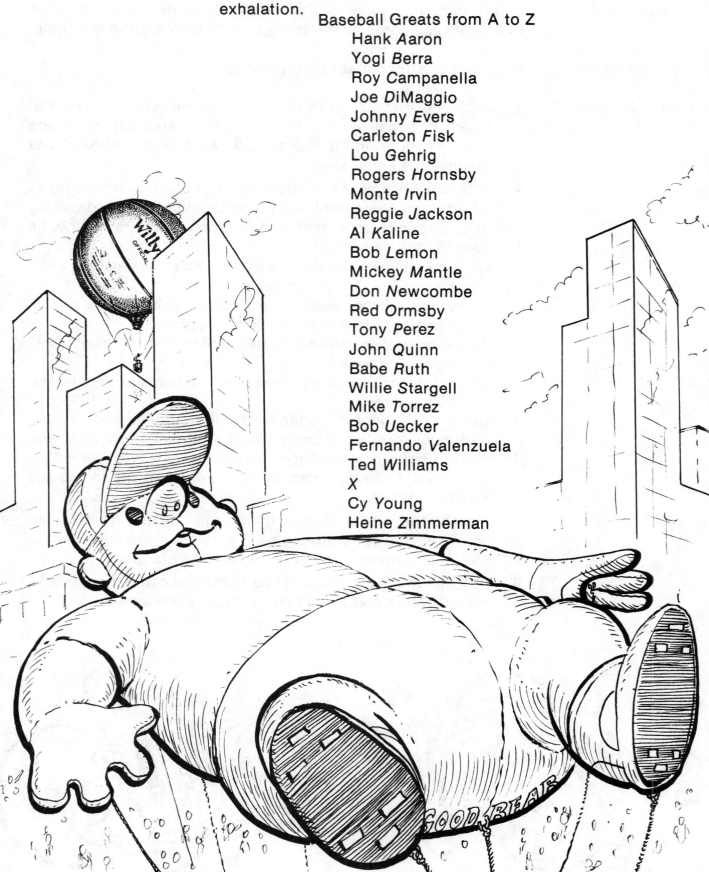

VARYING THE DESCRIPTION

OBJECTIVE: To reinforce the students' understanding of the four basic types of sentences in order to encourage sentence variation in writing.

MATERIALS: Four index cards per student, pencils

PROCEDURE:
1. Allow the class 20 to 25 minutes to observe a sports-related event (baseball game, football game, etc.) either in the school gym or on the playground. Make certain all students observe the same event.

2. After the observation, discuss the four basic sentence types with the students reminding the students that good writing often depends upon sentence variation. When reviewing, be sure to include:
   A. A declarative sentence makes a statement and usually ends in a period.
   B. An exclamatory sentence expresses strong feeling or surprise and ends with an exclamation point.
   C. An imperative sentence states a command or request and ends with a period.
   D. An interrogative sentence asks a question and ends with a question mark.

3. Once the students understand the four sentence types, distribute four index cards to each student. Ask each student to write one comment about the activity observed on each card. Each comment should be one of the four basic sentence types.

4. Collect the cards, shuffle them, and ask the students to stand. Read a statement to each student. If the statement is identified properly, the student remains standing.

5. Perhaps the teacher would like to make a contest out of this identification game and offer a blue ribbon as a reward.

THE SIX FACES OF DEFEAT AND VICTORY

OBJECTIVE: To exercise the muscles of the face in order to strengthen effective facial expressions.

MATERIALS: Baseball caps, hand mirrors, and pictures on the following pages

PROCEDURE:
1. Ask each student to look at the illustration entitled "Surprise" and to study the shape of the mouth, position of the eyebrows, and width of the eyes. Next, ask the students to try to copy the expression on their own faces. Use hand mirrors to check muscle tone and likeness.

2. Ask each student to look at the illustration entitled "Happy" and to again study the mouth, eyes, and eyebrows for shape. Ask each to copy the facial expression.

3. Continue this procedure for the rest of the pictures including "Overjoyed," "Tired," "Sad," and "Angry."

4. Ask each student to bring a couple of baseball cards to class. These cards should preferably be close-up shots. After selecting one to work with, each student should attempt to copy the facial expression on the baseball card. Remind the students to check the position of the jaw, the shape of the mouth, the line of the eyebrow, the eye width, etc.

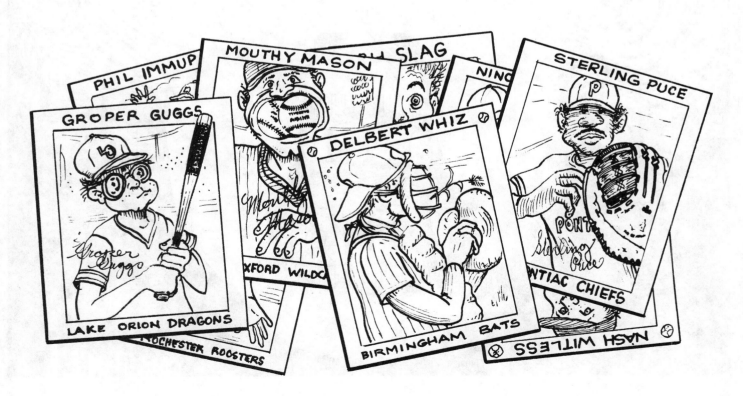

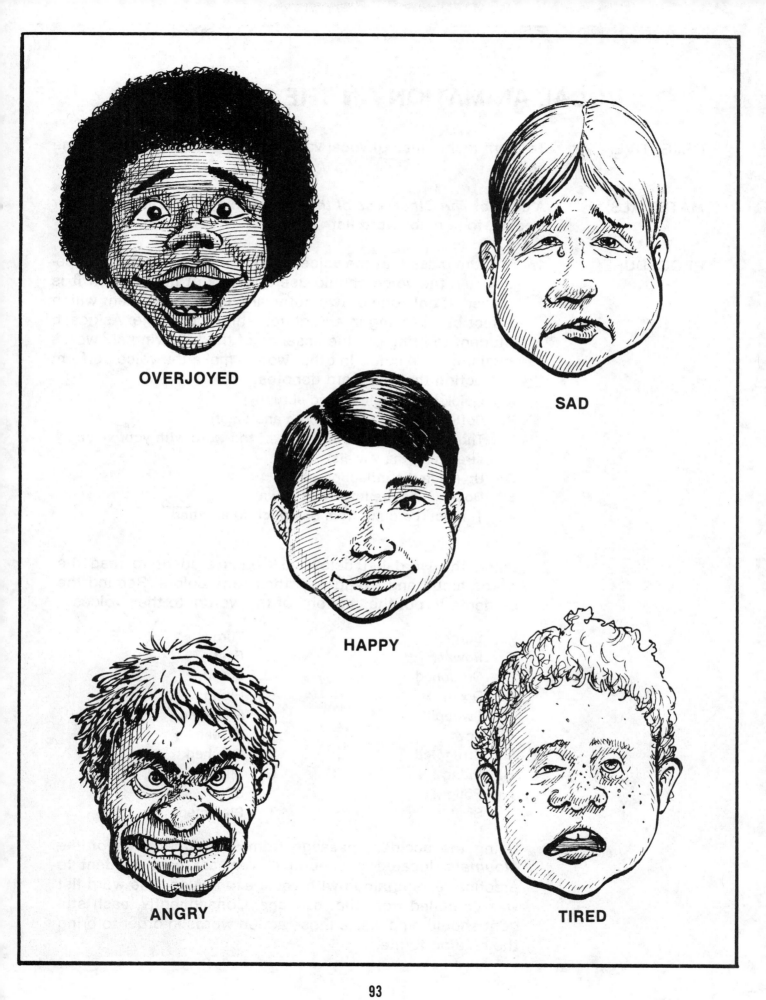

OVERJOYED

SAD

HAPPY

ANGRY

TIRED

VOCAL ANIMATION ON THE SLOPES

OBJECTIVE: To learn techniques of vocal variety through animation and tone color.

MATERIALS: A copy of *The Other Side of the Mountain* by E.G. Valens (Warner Books), tone color word list

PROCEDURE:
1. Tell the class that the voice is a musical instrument. Consequently, the voice should use a variety of notes when it is played. If only one or two notes are used, the student will in effect be speaking in an uninteresting monotone. Ask each student to bring out the essence of the following six words by using tone color. In other words, make the voice perform the action that the word denotes:

   A. Quick (say it quickly and abruptly)
   B. Soft (make the tone smooth and quiet)
   C. Thoroughly (cover every inch of the word with your voice by stretching the vowels)
   D. Up (slide the inflection up)
   E. Down (slide the inflection down)
   F. Turn (curl around from one pitch to another)

2. Using the word list below, ask each student to read the words aloud and exaggerate their tone colors. Remind the students to put the "action" of the word into their voices.

A.	Surge	K.	Turn
B.	Power	L.	Fast
C.	Crouched	M.	Lifted
D.	Down	N.	Flung
E.	Swooping	O.	Smashed
F.	Low	P.	Screamed
G.	Struggled	Q.	Crashed
H.	Flung	R.	Slid
I.	Fought	S.	Spun
J.	Shot	T.	Slammed

3. Using the accident passage from *The Other Side of the Mountain,* located in chapter eleven, ask each student to practice reading aloud with vocal expression. The word list was compiled from that passage. Consequently, each student should emphasize those action words in order to bring the reading to life.

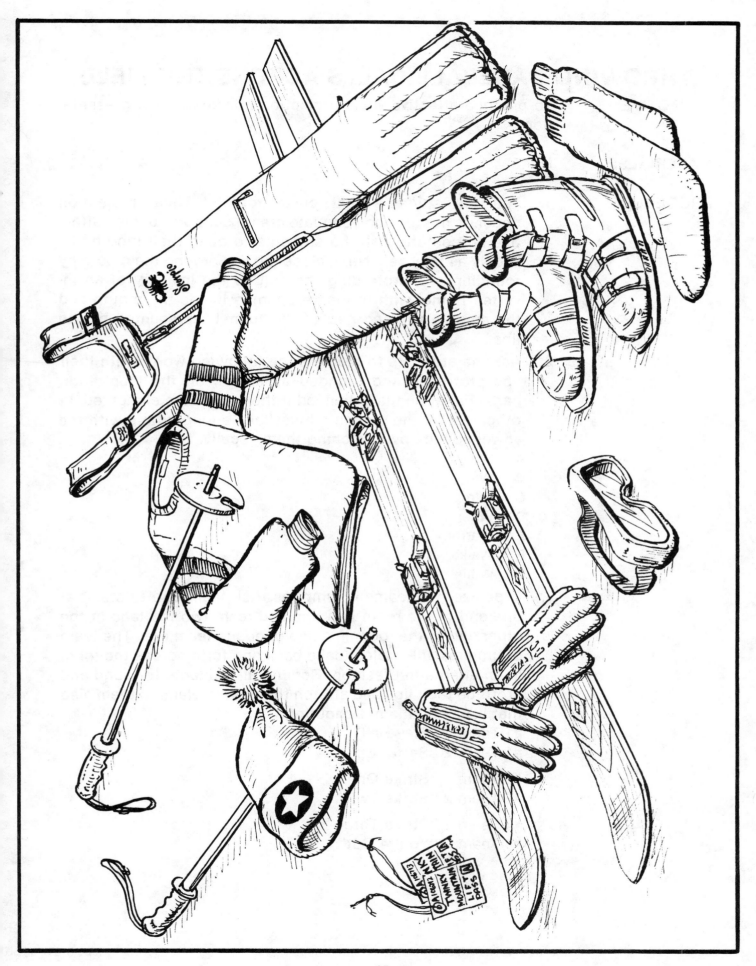

THROWING BASEBALL CALLS ACROSS THE FIELD

OBJECTIVE: To practice effective vocal projection prior to an oral presentation.

MATERIALS: None

PROCEDURE:

1. Tell the students that clear, forceful vocal projection depends not only on adequate breath support but also effective lip posture. Ask the students to open their mouths as widely as they can. Next, close the lips around the mouth by rounding and protruding them. (Use the imagery of an inverted funnel with the large opening inside the mouth and the small elongated part of the funnel represented by the lips.)

2. Ask the students to practice the following words with their lips protruded and rounded as shown on the illustration page. Projection is enhanced if the vowels are elongated. In other words, the students must take a longer time with the vowel sounds by stretching them vocally.
   A. We
   B. Will
   C. Win
   D. When
   E. Warren
   F. Walks
   G. Willie

3. Organize two teams of umpires. Ask team one to stand at one end of the room in a line and team two to stand at the other end of the room in a line opposite team one. The team of umpires will project calls back and forth across the room in an alternating fashion. Remind all students to round and protrude their lips and stretch the vowels. Remind them also that projection is not shouting.
   #1 Team 1 "Play Ball"
   #1 Team 2 "Batter Up"

   #2 Team 1 "Strike One"
   #2 Team 2 "Strike Two"

   #3 Team 1 "Strike Three"
   #3 Team 2 "You're Out"

#4 Team 1 "Foul Ball"
#4 Team 2 "Ball One"

#5 Team 1 "Ball Two"
#5 Team 2 "Ball Three"

#6 Team 1 "Ball Four"
#6 Team 2 "Time Out"

#7 Team 1 "You're Safe"
#7 Team 2 "Game Over"

4. If circumstances pose no problems, the teams could repeat the projecting of baseball calls from one team inside the room to the other team outside the room; from one team on one part of the playground to the other team on another part of the playground.

DARING DERBY DICTION

OBJECTIVE: To practice articulation in an effort to acquire clear diction.

MATERIALS: Word lists, table, chair, microphone, and audio recorder

PROCEDURE:
1. Tell the class that clear diction is concerned with the proper function of complete sounds. Many times a speaker cannot be understood because of mumbling and dropping word endings. In other words, the speaker is sloppy and careless with the articulation of each sound.

2. Ask the class to read the following one-syllable words aloud in unison. Remind them to exaggerate the articulation by sounding all word endings.
   A. Colt
   B. Horse
   C. Track
   D. Gate
   E. Start
   F. Odds
   G. Run
   H. Race
   I. Length
   J. Groom

3. Next, ask the class to read aloud the following two-syllable words using an overarticulated style on middle and ending consonants.
   A. Stable
   B. Furlong
   C. Jockey
   D. Saddle
   E. Bridle
   F. Trainer
   G. Homestretch
   H. Winner
   I. Circle
   J. Derby

4. Each word in the final list to be read aloud contains three, four or five syllables. Mumbling takes place most often when sounds are omitted from multi-syllable words.

A. Louisville
B. Kentucky
C. Handicap
D. Favorite
E. Spectators
F. Position
G. Thoroughbred
H. Victory
I. Celebration
J. Secretariat

5. Ask the class members to get into pairs. Each pair is responsible for writing an announcer's account of the Kentucky Derby using some or all of the words in the lists. The copy should begin with the words, "And they're off . . . ."

6. Each pair should role play the situation. One should be the announcer and the other should be the technician who runs the microphone and recorder. Remind the announcer to use an overarticulated style for this exercise.

RULES OF THE PODIUM GAME

OBJECTIVE: To acquire effective habits when speaking from a podium or in front of the class.

MATERIALS: A whistle, a podium or table, an easel for charts and bristol board, markers, and a stopwatch

PROCEDURE:

1. Explain the following rules of the podium game to the entire class:
   A. Don't lean on the podium, table or desk when speaking.
   B. Don't shift your weight back and forth from one foot to the other when speaking (stand flat on the floor with feet about six inches apart).
   C. Don't put your hands in your pockets and jangle your change, and don't fidget with note cards, jewelry or hair.
   D. Don't keep your head down in your notes preventing eye contact with your audience.
   E. Don't use note cards or manuscript pages that are not numbered.
   F. Don't turn your back on your audience and talk to your chart when using visual aids.
   G. Don't speak too fast by ignoring the use of the vocal pause.
   H. Don't mumble due to lazy lip action.
   I. Don't pass around handouts until your speech is finished.
   J. Don't lose spontaneous body action by planning gestures.

2. Ask each class member to prepare a three-minute oral report on how to play one of the following games: baseball, football, soccer, tennis, or hockey. Require each student to construct and use a chart during the informational speech. (Allow time for this to be completed.)

3. Review the rules of the Podium Game from one to ten. Tell the students that they will be allowed to speak as long as they do not break one of the ten rules. Tell them also that you will blow a whistle whenever they do break the rules. When the whistle blows, the student must sit down.

4. Ask a student to keep score as to how many seconds each speaker accomplishes before breaking a rule. A stopwatch should be used.

THE SEVENTH INNING STRETCH

OBJECTIVE: To free the body from tension prior to making an oral presentation via relaxation exercises.

MATERIALS: None

PROCEDURE:

1. Tell the students that they are going to take a seventh inning stretch. They have been sitting and watching a baseball game, and they need to stand up and stretch both arms away from the torso as far as they can. They are to stretch once again and yawn at the same time. (The exercise is most effective if each student stands up straight with both feet planted firmly on the ground about six inches apart.)

2. Next, the students should pretend they are baseball players sitting on the bench in the dugout. Ask them to hang their heads forward without support in their necks. Then, roll the head clockwise from the front, to the side, to the back, to the other side, and to the front again. (This head roll will release tension in the neck if the student is encouraged to let the head flop without much support.)

3. Put the class into four groups in order to do some stretch mimes. Group one is made up of pitchers, group two is filled with batters, group three is fielders, and group four is the umpires.

   A. Students in group one should each take a spot on the floor and designate it as a pitching mound. After picking up a ball, *in slow motion,* each student should stretch the pitching arm back as far as it is possible and then throw the ball. Execute the stretch—pitch ten times.

   B. Students in group two should each take a spot on the floor and designate it as home plate. After picking up a bat, *in slow motion,* each student should stretch the bat back as far as possible before swinging at the ball. Execute stretch—swing ten times.

   C. Students in group three should take a spot on the floor and designate it as the outfield. After looking up and seeing the fly ball, *in slow motion,* stretch arms up as far as you can as you reach as high as you can and catch the fly ball. Execute the reach—stretch ten times.

D. Students in group four should take a spot on the floor and designate it as first base. After watching the batter slide into first, *in slow motion,* move arms from a cross position and stretch out toward both sides as far as possible. Make the "safe" sign. Execute the safe—stretch ten times.

Unique!

OOPS, I GOOFED

OBJECTIVE: To introduce students to proofreading: skills, symbols, and the necessity for the process.

MATERIALS: Picture on the next page for each student, paragraph on page 106 for each student, paper, pencil

PROCEDURE:

1. Distribute a copy of the picture on the next page, and tell the students that there are ten mistakes in the picture. Allow students time to locate and circle these errors. The errors are:
   A. Player 24 wearing roller skates
   B. Truck on field
   C. Deer on field
   D. Player 17 holding soccer ball
   E. Player 17 wearing knight's helmet
   F. Blimp being held by string
   G. One player wearing baseball mitt
   H. Player 24 holding baseball bat
   I. One helmet has antenna
   J. One player holding yo-yo

2. Point out to the students that the visual skill they just used to find the errors in the picture is a form of proofreading. Proofreading is a visual, sometimes verbal review, of what has been written. All papers should be proofread prior to writing the final draft.

3. There are standard symbols that are used when proofreading any written materials. Present these editing symbols to the class:

   ¶ paragraph   ∿ transpose
   ∧ make a period   ◯ spell correctly
   ∧ add something   ≡ capitalize
   ∧ requires quotation marks   ɣ remove something
   ∧ requires comma   — lowercase letter

4. The teacher may wish to offer some helpful hints for proofreading to the children.
   A Use a different color ink to proofread so that corrections are legible.
   B. It is helpful to write your rough draft on every other line. When proofreading, you then have room to make corrections.
   C. Always have a dictionary handy when proofreading.

5. Distribute one copy of the paragraph on the next page to each student. Encourage students to use editing symbols to proofread the paragraph. (Each editing mark will be used at least twice in the paragraph.)

6. As an extension of this activity, the teacher may wish to assign a short sports-related paragraph to each student. Then allow students to trade papers and proofread one another's paragraph.

People can soar through the air like birds the sport that offers this thrill is hang-gliding. sometimes called self-soaring or surfing. Hang gliders are are made like kites that can support people. In order to hang glide, first, riders are harnessed into the glider Then the peoson holding kite is launched by downhull run or a jump from a cliff. While in the air the rider holds a bar, and shifts wait or Rolls to steer the kite the kite. You do not always need an airpalain to loom above the land. Safety and proper training are the most important conciderations when learning to hang glide glide. First, you must learn how to assemble your Glider to avoid equipment problems. Balance and preparing for take-off are vital safety precautions. Also it is important to make sure you adjust straps proproply timing and judging the wind are other factors to remember. It is vital to learn glider management and control Once you have mastered all of these skills you are ready to being a safe journey.

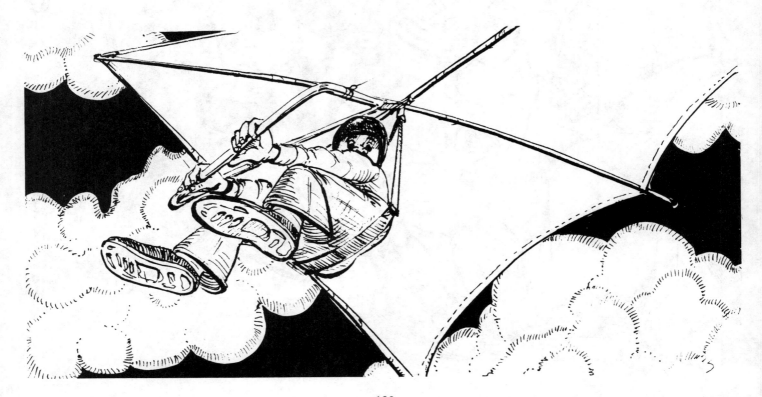

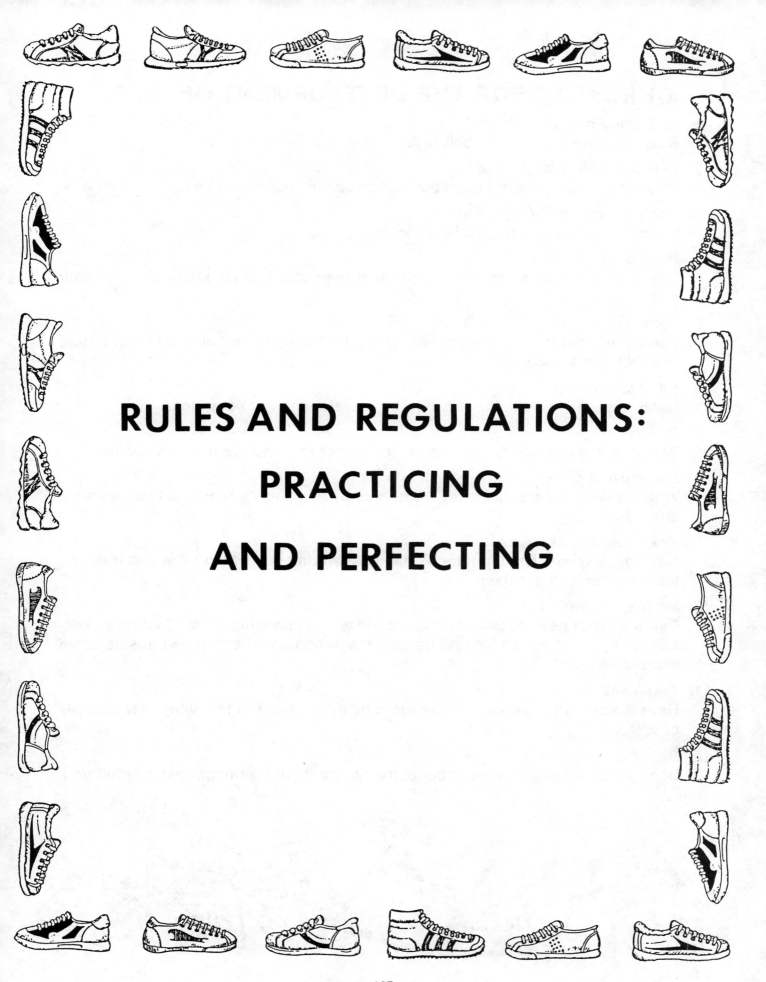

RULES AND REGULATIONS:

PRACTICING

AND PERFECTING

CHECKLIST FOR THE DEVELOPMENT OF IDEAS

1. *Be a good observer.*
Keep your eyes and ears open to what is going on around you.

2. *Let your mind play with ideas.*
Play with ideas by letting them bounce around in your mind in a nonsensical way.

3. *Don't be critical during ideation.*
Be sure not to discard any ideas too soon.

4. *Piggyback off others.*
Listen to the people around you and use their ideas to stimulate ideas of your own.

5. *Be fluent.*
Remember that the more ideas you generate, the more probable it is that one of them will be a good idea.

6. *Be open-minded.*
Don't allow narrow thinking to stop the development of your ideas.

7. *Daydream.*
Set aside time during the day to exercise your imagination by daydreaming.

8. *Know when to relax.*
When ideas are stale, get away from them by relaxing via tennis, biking, reading, etc.

9. *Keep a notebook of ideas.*
Be sure to keep a small notebook handy at all times in which to record ideas so that you don't forget them.

10. *Manipulate old ideas.*
Come up with new ideas by taking old ideas and changing them. Change can occur when things are added, subtracted, magnified, minified, turned upside down and pulled apart.

11. *Take risks.*
Have the courage to take risks by adopting new ideas and following new courses of action.

12. *Be curious.*
Don't be afraid to follow your curiosity by investigating things that interest you.

SELECTING THE TOPIC

1. *Assure interest.*
   Select a topic that interests you. You will be spending a great deal of time with the selection, and you may as well enjoy the topic.

2. *Pinpoint the ideas.*
   Make sure you are presenting one main idea in your report. An attempt to cover too much may lead to an incomplete treatment of any topic.

3. *Understand assignment.*
   Make certain you know all the expectations of the given assignment. Feel free to ask questions for clarification.

4. *Define purpose.*
   Decide whether you are writing to explain, defend a viewpoint, entertain, or inform. This will help to direct your research efforts.

5. *List questions.*
   Prepare a preliminary list of questions that you intend to research before going to the library. This saves time and directs research.

6. *Survey resources.*
   Before making a final decision about your topic, survey the available resources to make certain that at least five good sources are available.

7. *Don't forget cross-references.*
   Be certain to examine all cross-references during your preliminary library visit. Often, these references contain a wealth of fine materials.

8. *Know your audience.*
   Be aware of your audience. This awareness will make a difference in how you write your paper.

9. *Remember time and space.*
   Always keep time limits and space limits in mind when deciding about your paper. These considerations may help limit your topic.

10. *Keep topic specific.*
    Make certain that your topic selection can be researched thoroughly.

11. *Maintain positive attitude.*
    Know that you are doing a fine job and that you will present the topic in the best possible fashion.

12. *Verify topic.*
    After your preliminary research, it is a good idea to discuss your findings briefly with your instructor.

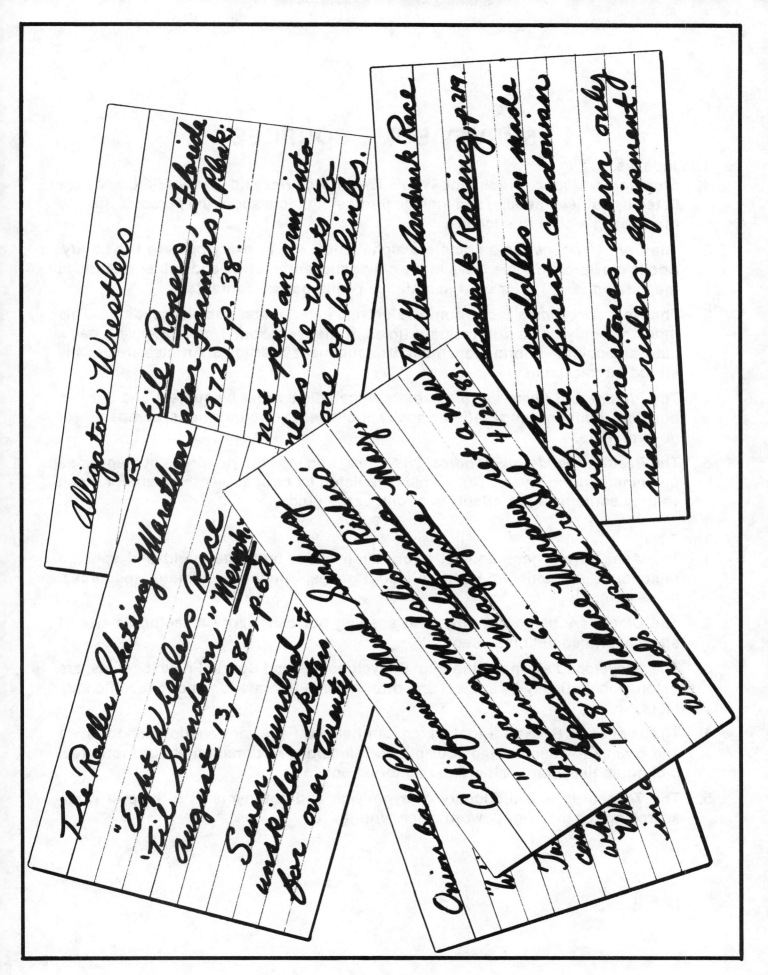

SURVEY SOME SOURCES

The Indexes:

1. *Biographical Indexes* including *Who's Who in America* and *Current Biography* are listed by subject (people) and include interesting facts about the person's life and the subject's path to success.

2. The *Card Catalogue* is a complete alphabetical list of every book in the library. Books are listed in three ways in the catalogue: author, title and subject. Cards in the catalogue will offer brief summaries of the books' contents.

3. The *New York Times Index* contains entries listed under subject headings. This index not only helps you locate articles in the *New York Times* by giving page, date, and column information, but it also summarizes articles. Articles are usually stored on microfilm.

4. The *Picture and Pamphlet files* are in alphabetical order by subject and contain booklets, bulletins, and leaflets usually published by organizations, companies or governments.

5. The *Readers' Guide to Periodical Literature* is an index to hundreds of magazines published during a year. The articles are listed by both subject and author. Each volume contains a list of abbreviations in the guide.

The Tools:

1. The *Atlas* offers geographical information about both the world and specific regions. It contains information about maps, products, climate, resources, measurements, etc.

2. The *Dictionary* helps not only with spelling but can clarify meanings, parts of speech, and sometimes usage.

3. The *Encyclopedias,* including Film Encyclopedias and Sports Encyclopedias, are listed alphabetically by subject and offer general information about specific subjects.

4. The *Language Book* is a tool which can help you answer questions about style and grammar when writing your paper. It includes information about footnotes, bibliographies, composition and punctuation.

5. The *Thesaurus* is a dictionary of synonyms and antonyms. It is helpful when searching for the "right" word when writing.

CHECKLIST OF WORDS OFTEN CONFUSED

1. *Accept*
   John accepted the trophy for the whole team.
   Except
   Every member of the team boarded the bus except John.

2. *Access*
   The team has access to the gymnasium.
   Excess
   Members of the team should not spend money in excess of what they make.

3. *Affect*
   The coach could affect the team positively.
   Effect
   The positive effect was caused by the coach.

4. *Are*
   The team's uniforms are in the locker room.
   Our
   We do not have our regular coach today.

5. *Costume*
   The band wore colorful costumes during half time.
   Custom
   It is the custom to sing the national anthem before the game.

6. *Desert*
   The empty stadium looked like a desert.
   Dessert
   There are no rich desserts on the training table.

7. *Its*
   The team has its first chance to win it all in five years.
   It's
   It's not impossible to take first place this year.

8. *Loose*
   His uniform is too loose.
   Lose
   Do not lose the stadium pass.

9. *Passed*
   The ball passed by first base at an incredible speed.
   Past
   Sports heroes of the past are all located in the *Who's Who.*

10. *Principal*
    The principal of the school has always supported organized sports.
    Principle
    The principles of good sportsmanship are not hard to learn.

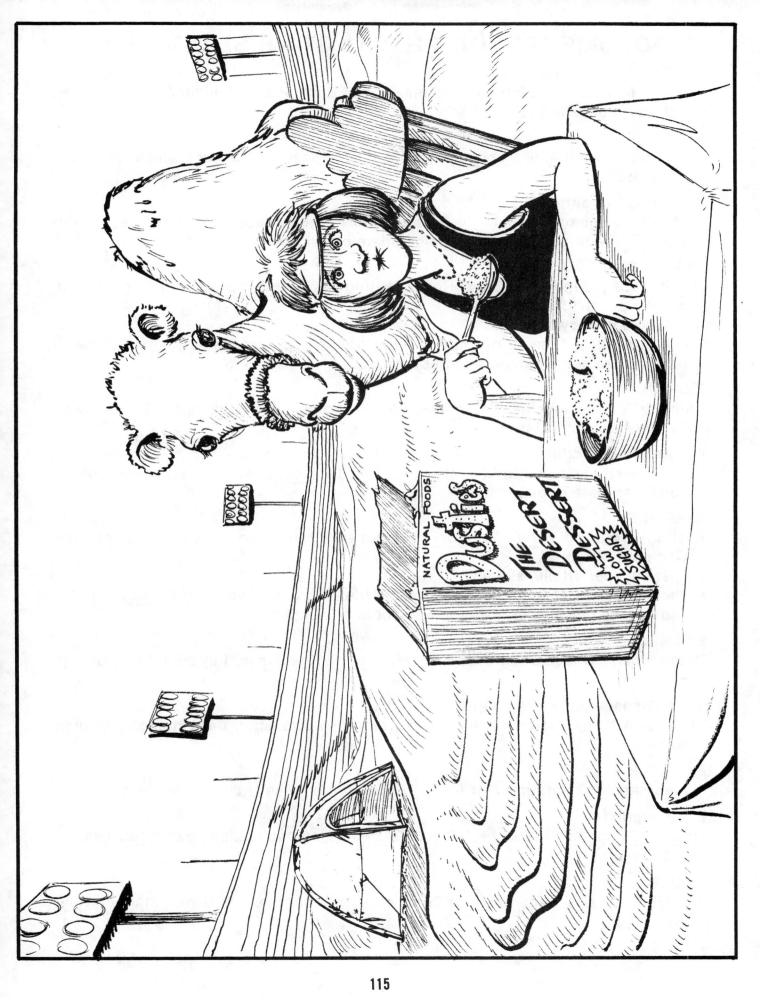

DOCUMENTATION CHECKLIST—BIBLIOGRAPHY

1. Book, one author

Author's last name, Author's first name. Title of Book. Place of publication: publisher, date of publication.

EXAMPLE

Dickmeyer, Lowell A. Skateboarding Is for Me. Minneapolis: Lerner Publications Company, 1978.

2. Book, two authors

Author I last name, Author I first name, and Author II first and last name. Title of Book. Place of publication: publisher, date of publication.

EXAMPLE

Olney, Ross R., and Chan Bush. Roller Skating. New York: William Morrow and Company, Inc., 1979.

3. Article in encyclopedia

"Name of article," Name of Encyclopedia, volume number, page number (Place of publication: publisher, date of publication).

EXAMPLE

"Athlete," Encyclopedia Britannica, vol. 2, pp. 614-615 (Chicago: Encyclopedia Britannica, Inc., 1954).

4. Book with editor

Editor's last name, editor's first name, ed. Title of Book. Place of Publication: publisher, date of publication.

EXAMPLE

Kesting, Ted, ed. The Outdoor Encyclopedia. New York: A. S. Barnes and Company,1957.

5. Newspaper article, signed

Author's last name, Author's first name. "Title of Article," Name of Newspaper, day and date of newspaper, page number, column number.

EXAMPLE

Bragg, Brian. "Chet's Catch Saves Tigers," Detroit Free Press, July 25, 1983, p. 1D, col. 5.

6. Newspaper article, unsigned

"Title of Article," Name of Newspaper, date of newspaper, page number, column number.

EXAMPLE

"Lions Shouldn't Let Sims Get Away," Detroit Free Press, July 25, 1983, p. 1D, col. 2.

7. Pamphlet

Title of Pamphlet. Sponsor of Pamphlet. Place of publication: publisher, year of publication.

EXAMPLE

Snowmobiles. U.S. Department of Commerce. Washington: U.S. Government Printing Office, 1969.

8. Weekly magazine article

Author's last name, Author's first name. "Title of Article," <u>Name of Magazine</u>, volume number, date of publication, page number.

EXAMPLE

Axthelm, Pete. "Money, Manners and Tennis," <u>Newsweek</u>, CII, July 4, 1983, p. 82.

9. Book, no author

<u>Name of Book</u>. Name of translator or editor. Place of publication: publisher, date of publication.

EXAMPLE

<u>The Inaugural Addresses of the American Presidents</u>. Annotated by Davis Newton Lott. New York: Holt Rinehart and Winston, 1961.

10. Story from anthology

Author of article last name, Author of article first name. "Title of Article." <u>Name of Book</u>. Edited by name of editor. Place of publication: publisher, date of publication.

EXAMPLE

Frost, Robert. "Stopping by Woods on a Snowy Evening." <u>Anthology of Children's Literature</u>. Edited by Edna Johnson, Evelyn R. Sickels and Frances Clark Sayers. Boston: Houghton, Mifflin Company, 1959.

SAMPLE BIBLIOGRAPHY

"Athlete," <u>Encyclopedia Britannica</u>, vol. 2, pp. 614-615 (Chicago: Encyclopedia Britannica, Inc., 1954).

Dickmeyer, Lowell A. <u>Skateboarding Is for Me</u>. Minneapolis: Lerner Publications Company, 1978.

Frost, Robert. "Stopping by Woods on a Snowy Evening." <u>Anthology of Children's Literature</u>. Edited by Edna Johnson, Evelyn R. Sickels and Frances Clark Sayers. Boston: Houghton, Mifflin Company, 1959.

Kesting, Ted, ed. <u>The Outdoor Encyclopedia</u>. New York: A. S. Barnes and Company, 1957.

"Lions Shouldn't Let Sims Get Away," <u>Detroit Free Press</u>, July 25, 1983, p. 1D, col. 2.

<u>Snowmobiles</u>. U.S. Department of Commerce. Washington: U.S. Government Printing Office, 1969.

DOCUMENTATION CHECKLIST—FOOTNOTES

1. Book, one author

[1] Author's first and last name, <u>Name of Book</u> (Place of publication: publisher, date of publication), page number.

EXAMPLE

[1] Lowell A. Dickmeyer, <u>Skateboarding Is for Me</u> (Minneapolis: Lerner Publications Company, 1978), p. 3.

2. Book, two authors

[1] Author I first and last name and Author II first and last name, <u>Name of Book</u> (Place of publication: publisher, date of publication), page number.

EXAMPLE

[1] Ross R. Olney and Chan Bush, <u>Roller Skating</u> (New York: William Morrow and Company, Inc., 1979), pp. 34-35.

3. Article in the encyclopedia

[1] "Name of Article," <u>Name of Encyclopedia</u> (Place of publication: publisher, date of publication), page number.

EXAMPLE

[1] "Athlete," <u>Encyclopedia Britannica</u> (Chicago: Encyclopedia Britannica, Inc., 1954), p. 614.

4. Book with editor

[1] First and last name of editor, ed., <u>Name of Book</u> (Place of publication: publisher, date of publication), page number.

EXAMPLE

[1] Ted Kesting, ed., <u>The Outdoor Encyclopedia</u> (New York: A. S. Barnes and Company, 1957), pp. 83-84.

5. Newspaper article, signed

[1] Author first and last name, "Title of Article," <u>Name of Newspaper</u>, date of newspaper, page number, column number.

EXAMPLE

[1] Brian Bragg, "Chet's Catch Saves Tigers," <u>Detroit Free Press</u>, July 25, 1983, p. 1D, col. 5.

6. Newspaper article, unsigned

[1] "Title of Article," <u>Name of Newspaper</u>, date of newspaper, page number, column number.

EXAMPLE

[1] "Lions Shouldn't Let Sims Get Away," <u>Detroit Free Press</u>, July 25, 1983, p. 1D, col. 2.

7. Pamphlet
[1] <u>Name of Pamphlet</u>, Sponsor of pamphlet (Place of publication: publisher, date of publication), page number.

EXAMPLE

[1] <u>Snowmobiles</u>, U.S. Department of Commerce (Washington: U.S. Government Printing Office, 1969), p. 1.

8. Weekly magazine
[1] Author's first and last names, "Title of Article," <u>Name of Magazine</u>, date of magazine, page number.

EXAMPLE

[1] Pete Axthelm, "Money, Manners and Tennis," <u>Newsweek</u>, July 4, 1983, p. 82.

9. Story from anthology
[1] Author of article first and last names, "Title of Article," <u>Name of Book</u>, editor's name (Place of publication: publisher, date of publication), page number.

EXAMPLE

[1] Robert Frost, "Stopping by Woods on a Snowy Evening," in <u>Anthology of Children's Literature</u>, ed. Edna Johnson, Evelyn R. Sickels and Frances Clark (Boston: Houghton, Mifflin Company, 1959), p. 1025.

10. Book, no author
[1] <u>Name of Book</u>, translator or editor (Place of publication: publisher, date of publication), page number.

EXAMPLE

[1] <u>The Inaugural Addresses of the American Presidents</u>, annotated by Davis Newton Lott (New York: Holt Rinehart and Winston, 1961), p. 43.

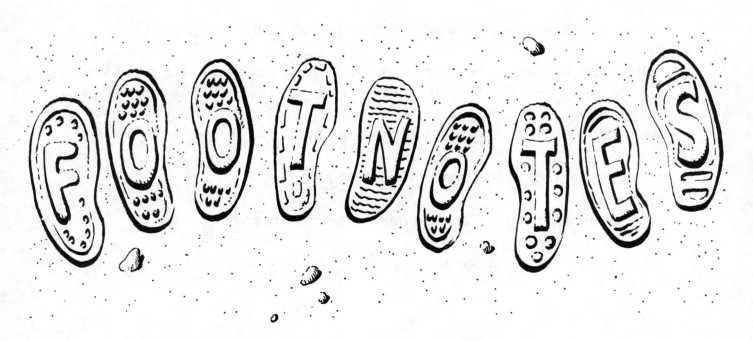

FIFTEEN QUESTIONS TO ASK
BEFORE THE FINAL DRAFT

1. *Purpose*
   Does the paper have a well-defined purpose and has the purpose been fulfilled in the paper?

2. *Title*
   Is the title short and does it give the reader an idea of what is to follow?

3. *Requirements*
   Have all required portions of the project been included (introduction, conclusion, footnotes, bibliography, etc.)?

4. *References*
   Have at least five different reference sources been used?

5. *Research question*
   Are all research questions answered in the paper?

6. *Documentation*
   Was the format for footnotes and bibliography checked to ascertain if it fulfills all class requirements?

7. *Sequence*
   Is the paper written in logical order?

8. *Punctuation*
   Has all punctuation including paragraphs, spelling, periods, commas, capitals, question marks and sentences been checked and rechecked?

9. *Format*
   Is the paper presented in proper format including margins written in ink or typed, page numbers and overall neatness?

10. *Graphs*
    Are all graphs and charts relevant and well-explained in the paper?

11. *Acknowledgements*
    Is the paper written in your own words, and has proper credit been given when using the thoughts and words of others?

12. *Final check*
    Has the paper been read aloud at least one time?

13. *Facts*
    Have facts and opinions been clearly delineated?

14. *Structure*
    Have sentence structure and sentence types been varied?

15. *Positive attitude*
    Am I proud of the final product?

ORGANIZATIONAL CHECKLIST

1. *Make cover attractive.*
   The *cover* of the report is attractive and includes an appealing title for the paper. The title is short, and it gives the reader an idea about the contents of the paper.

2. *Center the title.*
   The *title page* includes the appealing title and the author's full name. Author's name is right below the title. In the lower right-hand corner, the date and other required information should be listed.

3. *Display the topics.*
   The *table of contents* lists all the main headings from the outline and corresponding page numbers from the finished product.

4. *Create interest.*
   The *introduction* gives the reader an idea of what to expect in the paper. It creates interest and states the author's purpose.

5. *Present the research.*
   The *body* of the paper is the major portion of the presentation. It includes research, graphs, pictures, etc., all of which have been analyzed, proofread, and presented in an orderly fashion.

6. *Tie presentation together.*
   The *conclusion* summarizes the main points in the presentation. It ties the paper together.

7. *Order the footnotes.*
   The *footnotes* give credit to authors who supplied information for the report. They are ordered sequentially and are presented in standard format including author, title, publication facts, and page number.

8. *Credit the authors.*
   The *bibliography* includes a listing of all the sources used in the paper, even if the source was not used in footnotes. It is arranged alphabetically according to the authors' last names.

9. *Proofread.*
   All punctuation and spelling needs to be examined and corrected neatly. Make certain that all requirements for the paper have been fulfilled. Examine sentence structure and the general flow.

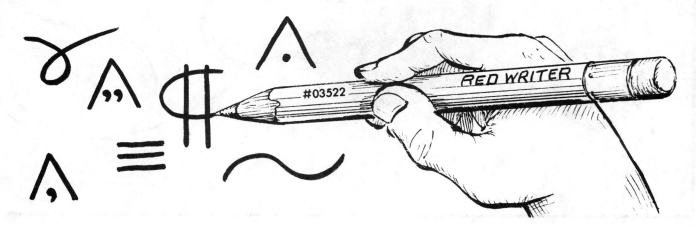

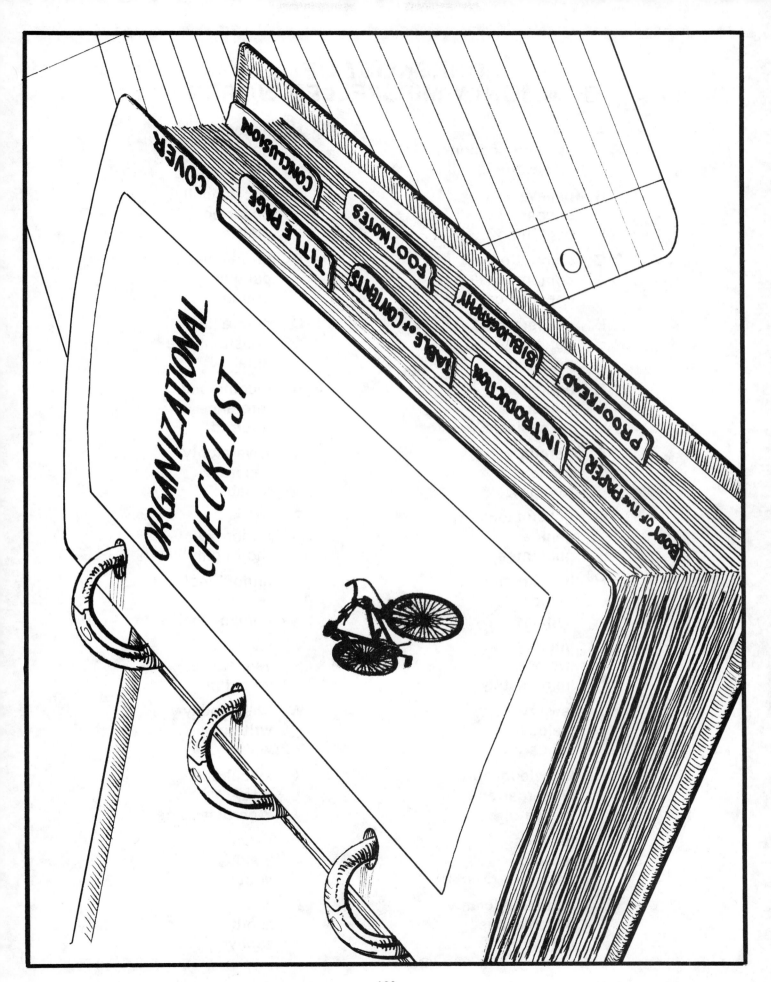

ORGANIZATIONAL CHECKLIST

COVER

TITLE PAGE

TABLE of CONTENTS

INTRODUCTION

BIBLIOGRAPHY

FOOTNOTES

CONCLUSION

PROOFREAD

BODY of the PAPER

CHECKLIST OF
COMMONLY MISSPELLED WORDS

A   a lot
    accommodation
    achievement

B   believe
    beggar
    beginning

C   committed
    comprehension
    conscience

D   desperately
    deficient
    decision

E   equipped
    emperor
    enthusiasm

F   February
    friend
    foreign

G   government
    genius
    guarantee

H   handkerchief
    heroes
    hygiene

I   interruption
    irrelevant
    immediately

J   jewelry
    jealousy
    January

K   knowledgeable
    kindergarten
    known

L   luxuries
    labeled
    literature

M   mathematician
    mischievous
    miniature

N   necessary
    naive
    nutrition

O   occasionally
    occurrence
    omitted

P   pronunciation
    parallel
    prairie

Q   quarrelling
    questionnaire
    quiet

R   recommend
    reference
    referred

S   sovereignty
    separate
    syllable

T   tragedy
    tomorrow
    thoroughly

U   undoubtedly
    usually
    unmanageable

V   vacuum
    vengeance
    verbatim

W   Wednesday
    writing
    weird

X   xylophone
    X-ray
    X-chromosome

Y   yacht
    yield
    yogurt

Z   zinc
    zenith
    zephyr

OVERCOMING THE FEAR OF PUBLIC SPEAKING

1. *Be prepared.*
   Start writing your report or speech early so that you have time to be thoroughly prepared.

2. *Practice before a live audience.*
   Ask your parents, brothers and sisters, and friends to listen to your speech before you officially give it.

3. *Tape your speech and play it back.*
   Evaluate yourself by taping your speech ahead of time and listening to it for logical flow.

4. *Get a good night's sleep.*
   A good night's sleep makes you feel good and confident.

5. *Practice in the very room you will be using.*
   Unfamiliarity breeds tension. Always try to practice your speech in the same environment in which you will give the speech.

6. *Relax prior to speaking.*
   Listen to music or do relaxation exercises to release tension that may build up prior to speaking.

7. *Concentrate on your message.*
   Don't think about yourself or your appearance. Only think about the words you are saying.

8. *Breathe deeply.*
   Diaphragmatic breathing relaxes the whole body.

9. *Find responsive faces in the audience.*
   Use eye contact on those audience members who seem attentive and friendly.

10. *Use bodily action to relieve tension.*
    Gestures can release tension that builds up as your speech proceeds.

11. *Be positive.*
    Know that you are doing the very best job that you can do. Be proud of it.

12. *Smile.*
    A smile can make an anxious moment become friendly.

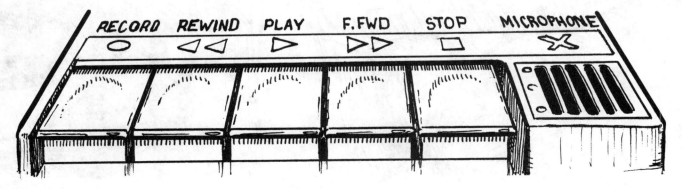

CHECKLIST FOR EFFECTIVE SPEECHMAKING

1. *Use diaphragmatic breathing.*
   Deep breathing relaxes the body while providing good support for the voice.

2. *Keep your head erect.*
   Decrease tension on the vocal cords by keeping your head erect at a normal eye level.

3. *Beware lazy lips.*
   Poor lip articulation can cause you to mumble and consequently be a poor communicator.

4. *Use a variety of vocal notes.*
   Monotones result when the speaker uses only one or two vocal tones. This is very boring to the listener's ear.

5. *Conversational quality is important.*
   Always talk *with* rather than *at* your audience.

6. *Use eye contact.*
   Eye contact with the audience is necessary for credibility and sincerity.

7. *Number all note cards.*
   Always number your note cards so that if they get mixed up they can easily be put back in order.

8. *Keep arms at your side.*
   Don't allow your hands to "play with" your note cards or jangle coins in your pockets.

9. *Stand up straight.*
   Never slouch on the podium, but rather stand evenly on your two feet.

10. *Never plan gestures.*
    Let all gestures arise spontaneously out of your involvement with your material.

11. *Use facial expressions.*
    Allow your face to reflect what your mouth is saying.

12. *Smile.*
    Make sure your face is pleasant to look at by avoiding expressions of pain or fear.

13. *Avoid misusing the voice.*
    Never misuse your voice by shouting, cheering or singing uncontrollably prior to public speaking.

CHECKLIST OF OFTEN MISPRONOUNCED WORDS

1. *Film*
   This word has only one syllable, not two.

2. *Giant*
   This word has two syllables, not one.

3. *Often*
   This word has two syllables, not one.

4. *Picture*
   This word is not pronounced "pitcher."

5. *Cabinet*
   This word has three syllables, not two.

6. *Sherbet*
   This word does not have an "r" in the second syllable.

7. *Restaurant*
   This word has three syllables, not four.

8. *Athletics*
   This word has three syllables, not four.

9. *Prescription*
   This word begins with the prefix "pre" not "per."

10. *Temperature*
    This word has four syllables, not just three.

11. *Cemetery*
    This word has four syllables, not three.

12. *Veterinarian*
    This word contains six syllables, not just five.

13. *Across*
    This word does not end with a "t."

14. *Ask*
    This word is not pronounced "ax."

15. *Ten and Pen*
    The words "ten" and "pen" are not pronounced "tin" and "pin."

16. *Relevant*
    This word is not pronounced "revelant."

17. *Chimney*
    This word is not pronounced "chimbley."

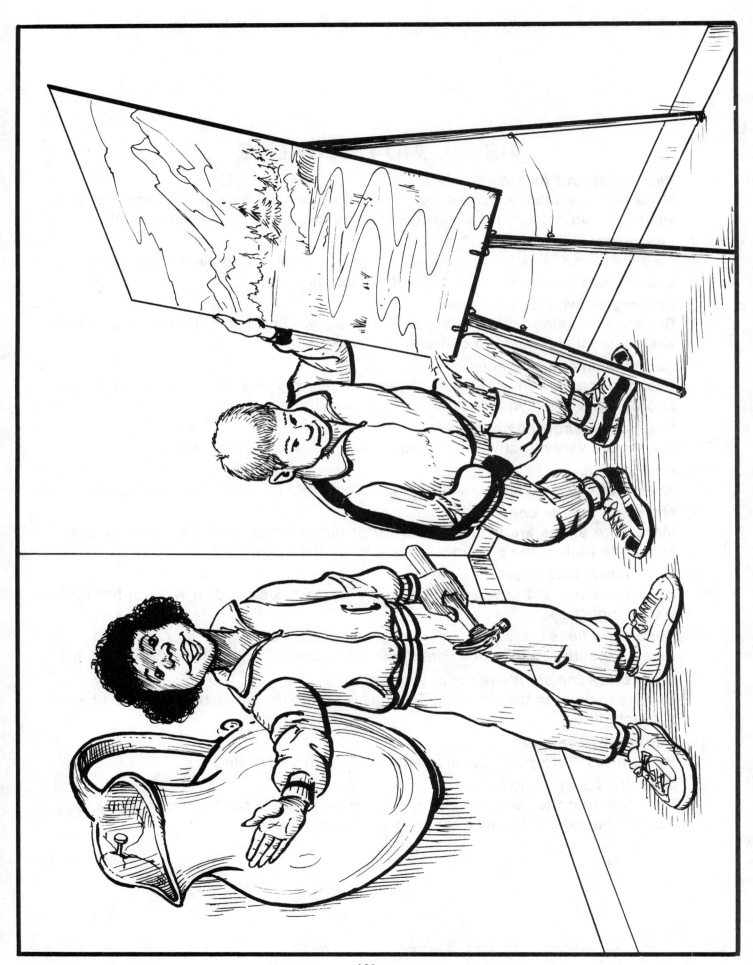

VISUAL AID CHECKLIST

1. *Use chalkboard for simple information.*
   Make sure the chalkboard is used when there is a need for a simple, spontaneous visual aid. Do not use the chalkboard for complicated figures or illustrations.

2. *Live models are risky.*
   Be alert to the possible emergencies involved when using live models as visual aids. People are often late, sick and/or unpredictable.

3. *Use one or two ideas per chart.*
   Beware of making charts and graphs too busy. Limit each chart to one or two ideas. Visual aids that are cluttered are not effective.

4. *Cartoons and photographs can be useful.*
   Use cartoons when you want to add humor to your presentation, and use photographs when you want to add emotionality.

5. *Graphs can show comparisons.*
   Graphs are very effective if you want to show comparisons visually.

6. *Be accurate.*
   Always prepare models to scale for accuracy. Include a visible legend or key.

7. *Make last minute checks.*
   Make sure slides are in the proper order just prior to your presentation. Also, check the bulb in the projector and prefocus the material.

8. *Don't reveal aids ahead of time.*
   Keep the visual aid covered until you are going to use it, or it will not have full visual impact.

9. *Keep sight lines clear.*
   Be sure that the podium does not block the audience's sight line of the visual aid.

10. *Don't block the sight lines with your body.*
    Be sure to point to the aid with the hand closest to the aid so that you won't block the sight line.

11. *Don't talk to your aid.*
    Be sure to talk to your audience and not to your visual aid.

12. *Clear the background area.*
    Take care that the walls around your speaking area are not filled with distracting visuals that could take interest away from your visual aid.

AUDIOVISUAL CHECKLIST

1. *Motion Picture Projector*

   All motion projection equipment is comprised of a series of still pictures. However, when shown in rapid motion succession on a film projector, film creates the illusion of motion. Motion pictures are shown on 8 or 26 mm projectors. A motion picture can take an audience to another culture, another time, or another world.

2. *Filmstrips and Filmstrip Projector*

   A filmstrip is a strip of film that presents still pictures (usually in a sequence). Often, there are printed explanations on the filmstrip, or the strip can be accompanied by sound or voice narration. The filmstrip can be presented on an individual or large group projector. Filmstrips are easily made by students of all ages. A student may wish to visually portray a procedure or demonstrate an idea while presenting research. Filmstrips are a perfect vehicle for these visual presentations.

3. *Microfilm*

   Microfilm is a "microform" (materials photographically reduced in size) that stores pages of magazines, newspapers, documents, and pamphlets on film. Microfilm provides easy storage and quick access to these documents. The student researcher might use microfilm in conjunction with the *Readers' Guide to Periodical Literature* to read newspaper and magazine accounts of current topics. Microfilm is used with a reader that enlarges the film for easy access.

4. *Overhead Projectors*

   Overhead projectors are still projection materials that focus attention upon enlarged projection aids. These aids may be student or commercially prepared. Overhead projectors enlarge productions and project them on a screen or wall. Because motion is not a factor, these projectors can allow for speed control and consequently complete comprehension. They are helpful in student research and presentation because charts and graphs can be projected and explained. Student art and writing can be discussed, and attention is easily focused.

5. *Slides and Slide Projectors*

   Slides are small picture still projection materials which present visual representations that can be projected to large groups. Making slides is as simple as using a camera. However, slides differ from instant developed photos in that slides are framed. A projector helps focus attention to the slide and thus slides are helpful for any research presentation where visual representation is necessary.

6. *Video Equipment*

   A video tape is a magnetic tape that records BOTH sound and picture. Video equipment records and plays back on television equipment. Video equipment can be used in research for observation, simulation, or relatively easy transmission from expert to classroom. Video tapes might be irreplaceable for the student who cannot overcome stage fright.

CHECKLIST FOR PHYSICAL IMPRESSION
WHEN SPEAKING

1. *Don't wear sunglasses.*
   Never wear sunglasses or darkly tinted lenses when speaking before a group due to the fact that it interferes with eye contact.

2. *Wear comfortable clothes.*
   Uncomfortable and tightly fitting clothes will interfere with your concentration.

3. *Don't chew gum.*
   Never chew gum while making a speech. It is rude and it also impedes articulation.

4. *Beware of jangling jewelry.*
   Bracelets, pendants and watches that knock against the podium are distracting.

5. *Clothes should be clean and neat.*
   Check buttons, zippers, cuffs and collars before getting up in front of an audience.

6. *Keep your hair out of your face.*
   Never allow your hair to fall into your face because it will annoy the audience.

7. *Don't continually shift your weight.*
   Stand with your weight evenly distributed so that you don't continually shift your weight.

8. *Don't wear distracting clothes.*
   Never wear clothing that will distract from your speech, such as T-shirts with slogans.

9. *Personal pronouns require eye contact.*
   Always look directly at the audience when you say "I," "we," "you" or "us" in order to maintain sincerity.

10. *Let your whole body react.*
    Allow your whole body to react to your material, including your face.

11. *Don't get too close to microphones.*
    Never lean into a microphone and cause it to pop.

12. *Position your arms at your sides.*
    Whenever you are not gesturing, allow your arms to hang naturally at your sides.

DO:

DON'T :

CHECKLIST FOR VOCAL INTERPRETATION OF ORAL REPORTS

1. *Experience the imagery.*
   Experience the imagery firsthand by seeing, feeling, tasting and touching everything you say you see, feel, taste or touch.

2. *Make the words live.*
   Use the tone color of the adjectives and adverbs, and do with your voice what the words say is being done.

3. *Use a variety of rates.*
   Statistics and technical material are spoken at a slower rate than narrative or transitional material.

4. *Inflect sentence endings properly.*
   Questions end with a rising inflection whereas statements end with a downward inflection.

5. *Use the vocal pause for emphasis.*
   A vocal pause prior to a phrase calls attention to it whereas a vocal pause after a phrase strengthens its effect.

6. *Never laugh at your own comedy.*
   Always deliver your own funny lines in a serious manner in order not to reduce the incongruity.

7. *Always "plant" humorous material.*
   A vocal pause, a space of silence, just prior to humorous material plants the joke in the ears of the audience.

8. *Vocally always credit material written by others.*
   When quoting a poem, joke or passage, always identify the author.

9. *Use enough volume.*
   Make sure the last person in the last seat can hear you.

10. *Check pronunciations.*
    Always check the proper pronunciations of words within your oral report or speech, including names of people and foreign cities and countries.

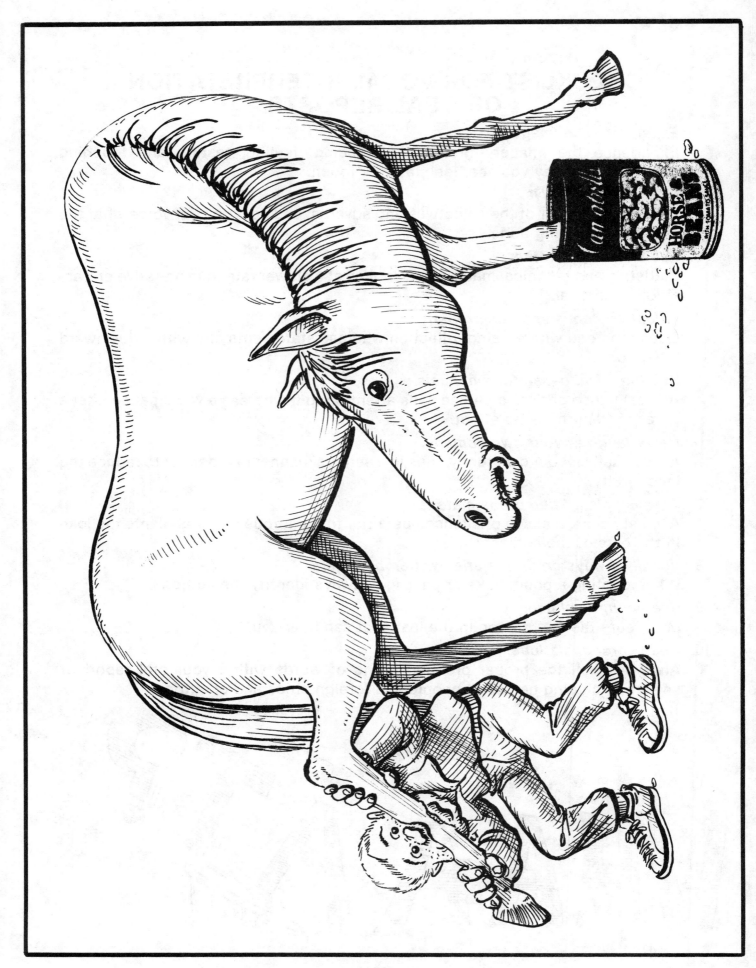

RESEARCH WORKOUT GLOSSARY

1. *Alliteration*
   Alliteration is a form of figurative language in which beginning consonant sounds are repeated.
   EXAMPLE: Baseballs bounce beautifully before breakfast.

2. *Antonym*
   An antonym is a word that is opposite in meaning to another word.
   EXAMPLE: amateur/professional.

3. *Bibliography*
   A bibliography is an alphabetical listing of all written materials used in research. The listing includes authors' names, book titles, and publication information.

4. *Colloquialism*
   A colloquialism is an expression that is often used in everyday, informal conversation. It is not usually accepted in formal speaking or writing.
   EXAMPLE: "I can't stand it" meaning I am not able to tolerate something.

5. *Declarative sentence*
   A declarative sentence makes a statement and usually ends in a period.
   EXAMPLE: Johnny may play baseball today.

6. *Exclamatory sentence*
   An exclamatory sentence is a sentence that expresses a strong feeling or surprise. It ends with an exclamation point.
   EXAMPLE: I can't believe we won again today!

7. *Homonym*
   A homonym is a word that has the same pronunciation as another word but has a different meaning and a different spelling.
   EXAMPLE: night/knight.

8. *Hyperbole*
   A hyperbole is a figure of speech in which exaggeration is used to create an effect.
   EXAMPLE: I am hungry enough to eat a horse.

9. *Idiom*
   An idiom is a figure of speech that is peculiar to a given language. It cannot always be translated literally.
   EXAMPLE: "I give up" meaning I surrender.

10. *Imperative sentence*
    An imperative sentence states a command or request. It ends with a period.
    EXAMPLE: Open the door.

11. *Interrogative sentence*
    An interrogative sentence asks a question and ends with a question mark.
    EXAMPLE: What time does the game begin?

12. *Metaphor*

    A metaphor is an analogy. That is, it is a comparison of two objects. The comparison does not use the words "as" or "like."
    EXAMPLE: The snow on the ski slope was powdered sugar.

13. *Onomatopoeia*

    Onomatopoeia is the use of words to suggest sounds.
    EXAMPLE: "bang," "crash," "bow-wow."

14. *Paraphrase*

    To paraphrase is to restate an idea using different words and combinations of words.
    EXAMPLE: "Getting the last word" might be paraphrased to mean having the final say in a matter.

15. *Personification*

    Personification is giving human characteristics to something that is not human.
    EXAMPLE: The baseball cried when it was hit.

16. *Plagiarism*

    Plagiarism is a form of theft in the literary world. It is stealing the thoughts or words of another person.

17. *Point of View*

    Point of view is the manner in which material is presented to the audience.

18. *Simile*

    A simile is a comparison of two objects. This analogy uses the words "as" or "like."
    EXAMPLE: Her eyes are as blue as the sky.

19. *Synonyms*

    A synonym is a word that has a meaning that is similar to the meaning of another word.
    EXAMPLE: frightened/scared.

20. *Thesaurus*

    A thesaurus is a listing of synonyms and antonyms for many words.

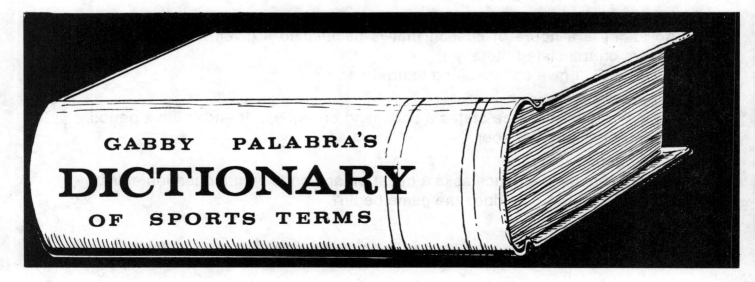

GABBY PALABRA'S
DICTIONARY
OF SPORTS TERMS